Spirit *Life Goes On*
Children

Charmaine Wilson

FONTAINE
— PRESS —

Copyright © 2009 Charmaine Wilson
Published by Fontaine Press
P.O. Box 948, Fremantle
Western Australia 6959
www.fontainepress.com

National Library of Australia Cataloguing-in-Publication data
Author: Wilson, Charmaine
Title: Spirit children : life goes on / Charmaine Wilson.
Edition: 1st ed.
ISBN: 9780980672909 (pbk.)
Subjects: Spiritualism.
           Children--Death.
           Bereavement.
           Grief
 Dewey Number: 133.9013

Cover photo by Melissa Stanley

For more information about the author,
please visit: www.charmainewilson.com.au

Dedicated to The Spirit Children.

Acknowledgements

My eternal love and loyalty to the spirit world for its teachings and love.

To my spirit family: Martin, Crystal, Mervyn, and Dad, recently joined by Mum and Rebmen. I miss you all every day, but feel your light stronger than ever now.

To my partner, Patrick, who makes life so much easier and makes me see reason when I think there is none. To my two sons, Alan and Jack, for accepting what is and for loving me unconditionally.

To my remaining family few. Thank you for your constant support.

To my faithful assistants, Deb and Trevor, you are the cogs in the wheels of *Spirit Whispers* – Thank you.

To Fontaine Press for believing in me when so many didn't. Thank you for your faith.

To the parents who shared their stories in this book. My eternal love. May we have found a way to make this harshest of journeys a little easier for others.

To the Spirit Children - I hear you, I feel you , I see you - and I will continue to share your love with all who come in search of hope.

Prologue

Martin
(3.3.1962 - 2.4.1982)

My mother was the first bereaved mother I ever met.

On a mild Australian autumn day in 1982, my mother beckoned me into her sewing room and shut the door behind me. I stood in the small room with my baby daughter on my hip and looked enquiringly at my mother's face. It was etched with worry as she confided she had been having dreadful feelings and was sure someone in the family would soon die.

She had a folder in her hand and pulled out the family wills, insisting I look at them and remember where they were kept. Like any seventeen-year-old, I told her she was overreacting. It was her imagination. No one was going to die. I didn't want to contemplate losing my mother. We'd always had a close relationship and had become even closer since Crystal had been born. There had been the usual family arguments; the shock of being a grandmother at thirty-seven must have rocked mum, but our family was solid. I tried to alleviate her fears with all types of suggestions, but still she insisted. The look on her face filled me with fear. I put our conversation out of my mind and did not think about it until exactly one week later.

My twenty-year-old brother, Martin, was killed instantly when a car failed to stop at a stop sign and collided with his motorcycle. My brother didn't stand a chance. One life wiped out in a split second.

When a tragedy such as this impacts a family, it is akin to dropping a bomb in the middle of the family home. The shock and grief explode and each member is thrown in a different direction. We can only ever be sure of our own feelings in this situation. When my brother died, the grief enveloped me in relentless black waves. There was no break from the force of this grief. There was no escape. Every day for months was like waking up to the same nightmare: my brother was dead. Nothing was going to bring him back. Praying, begging and bargaining with God proved useless. His time was over and there were no more chances to say anything to him.

My parents had separated twelve years earlier and both had remarried. Dad had another daughter and three sons and my mum had another son. We grew up with mum, my stepfather and my younger brother and spent every other weekend with my dad. So it was quite an extended family that felt the impact of this tragic event.

We all get wrapped up in our own feelings at a time like this, and we can forget that others may not grieve the way we do. Some feel guilty, others feel robbed and others just cease to feel at all. I felt guilt.

My brother was a noisy person whose energy hit the room way before he did. He had mum wrapped around his finger; however, his charms were lost on me. I loved him but we ignited each other's fuses quite quickly and would often have screaming matches, much to the embarrassment and amusement of our peers. He was popular with all my friends and Crystal's father. Therefore, I had the pleasure of Martin's company everyday. He had recently stopped living at home and had spent a great deal of time sleeping on my couch. The day he died was to be his first day living with his girlfriend in a small flat.

I was not so sure I had been the best sister I could have been. I now understand that we learn how to react to the outside world from our siblings. Being so close in age set off a natural competition between us. It is normal to fight and test our siblings. You only need to look at a litter of puppies, always fighting and tumbling, to understand that human siblings are the same. I did not know this then and was devastated I had not been more patient.

We were lucky to have Crystal. Only four months old at the time, she became a small and delightful healing balm for the whole family. Mum grew incredibly close and transferred all the love she reserved for Martin onto her.

I often wondered how mum really felt about losing Martin. They were so close. He would tease and cuddle her. In fact, he was the only one of us she would cuddle. His personality demanded physical attention and he usually got what he wanted.

Although I know she missed Martin dreadfully, she rarely showed her emotion regarding his death. She somehow kept herself aloof and grew in emotional strength. Her body, however, absorbed the grief and her lungs, plagued with asthma her whole life, began a slow deterioration.

She used her emotional strength to prop me up and hold the family together. Mum was an example of quiet dignity in the face of disaster. She instinctively knew how to lift herself. She took up bike riding, which would have cleared her airways and Chi energy lines, and she was always mindful of her diet. Without realising it, she was maintaining a high vibrational energy level. She knew in her heart that she had been the best mum she could. I am sure this went a long way in keeping her standing tall.

Instead of following mum's lead of good nutrition and exercise, I decided to indulge in low vibrational behaviour. I smoked pot and cigarettes, fought constantly with Crystal's dad and generally felt sorry for myself.

Despite losing her first-born son, mum remained the same with me and I am sure she was also the same with my younger brother. She didn't put Martin on a pedestal. She kept his memory alive for a while but didn't waste time openly on the 'what ifs' and the 'if onlys.' She cleaned out his little flat in silence and I am sure she cried much more than I will ever know. She kept one small bag of his belongings and everything else was disposed of. She made a tape of his songs and played it constantly in her little car. My stepfather, who was an artist, painted his portrait and she hung it proudly on the wall.

On the first anniversary of Martin's death, she drove to the accident site at the exact time of his death to see if the driver of the car had been lying when he claimed the sun was in his eyes and that he had not seen my brother. He had been. My mother told me this almost twenty years after she drove there. She never said a word before that.

It was almost as if mum had a private grief even though she talked about Martin a lot to me. I shared my grief with anyone who would listen. There were no mediums in Australia in 1982. There were very few grief counsellors and the only books on this subject were generally religiously based. We were not a religious family, nor were we truly spiritual, but we did believe in other worlds and as a family felt that there was much more to the little coincidences than others may have. We noticed the song on the radio just as we would be talking about Martin or the person in the crowd who for a split second smiled in exactly the same way. We knew he was around. I remember using the ouija board to locate him with success. My brother smoked pot as well and always called a joint a J. We all fell about laughing when we asked him if he was okay and the cup spelt out: "I would love a J."

The tragic death of a close loved one causes you to ask questions and starts to open you up spiritually. When we viewed his body, we all noticed that it was only his body and decided on that day his soul was still travelling. It was one of the hardest tasks we had to undertake as a family. For a brief period, I used Martin's death as a crutch and often played 'poor me' when I wished to avoid confrontations. It was mum who berated me and told me not to be so morbid and to move forward.

So we did. The seasons rolled a full circle and time stopped for no one nor did our lives. Like the seasons, I also changed. I changed houses and fought with Crystal's dad. I took up guitar playing and we fought over the guitar. I had cancer removed from my nose and fought my ego about my lost looks.

Crystal grew more enchanting daily and started to talk. I changed houses again and moved closer to my mum. When autumn rolled around again and another year passed, my time with Crystal's dad also ended.

I added drinking to my addiction list and went wild for a time. My mum became my lifeline and access visits were handed down to another generation.

Martin drifted into the past as we ventured into the future, time inching slowly forward.

Crystal
(13.11.1981 - 28.6.1986)

I was the second bereaved mother I ever met.

On a cool winter's night in 1986, I woke from a dream in a lather of sweat. My heart rate was accelerated, my breathing fast and my face wet with tears.

In the dream, I was with my partner and another friend, who was holding a baby. Somehow I knew the baby belonged to us all. I was holding Crystal's hand. We walked through an archway into a grassy foyer, and then through another archway. There were people everywhere. The ground sloped upwards, and everyone was walking up the incline. They all looked like they were sleep-walking, even my friend and my partner. Suddenly I felt Crystal disappear. Frantic, I tore back the way we had come to try to find her.

"Have you seen a little girl, about this high, with sandy brown hair?" I begged a passerby. He just shook his head. I went back through the second archway and saw a hippie we had passed earlier and I repeated my question:

"Have you seen a little girl with sandy brown hair - about this high?"

"No man," he answered solemnly, "she's gone." Distressed, I pleaded with him, "You must remember! We just passed by with her!"

The hippy just looked me in the eyes. "No man, she's gone," he said.

I leapt out of bed and ran to my daughter's bedroom. Everything was in place. Her bed was neatly made and her surprise Barbie clothes ready to present to her lay upon it. I was hyperventilating and steadied myself by sitting on her bed. My mind grappled between the dream and reality until I realised Crystal was still at her father's on an access visit. She was due home in a week. It was only a dream. Why then was my heart still thumping like a bass drum in my chest?

Anxiety began to gnaw at my stomach as I convinced myself to go back to bed. I lay in the dark trying to sleep but fear had crept into my heart and made itself comfortable. The next day, I relayed the dream to my live-in partner and my mum. They both assured me it was only a dream. When our new puppy went missing for a few worrisome hours, I decided the dream was about the pup.

I called my daughter that evening and she begged me to come and get her. The fear in my heart stretched and yawned and let me know it was waking up.

The following evening, my four-year-old daughter was a passenger in the car her drunken father was driving. He lost control, the car rolled and my daughter was knocked unconscious. Her tongue blocked her airways and she suffocated to death.

Our Crystal was gone forever.

The police woke me the following morning to relay the news.

I stared at them stupidly. Their mouths were moving and everything seemed to slow down. 'Fatally injured' were the words they were saying. It would not compute.

"Did she lose a limb?" I asked. They backed away after ensuring I was not alone. My partner had come to the door to see what the trouble was and held me tightly. I couldn't understand. What had happened to Crystal?

Her grandfather spoke the words I finally understood when I called her father's house: Crystal was dead.

When the bomb hit my home this time, the blast deafened me as it set off screaming sirens. It was my own screaming I could hear.

Nothing prepares you for the loss of a child. No pain can compare. Losing Martin had been so hard and the pain I felt was unbearable, but losing Crystal was horrific. My mother rushed to my side, but this time I could not draw any comfort from her presence or anyone else's. Nothing and everything was what I felt. I was disconnected from the universe. Wave after wave of grief knocked me until I began to sink lower into a black sea of pain.

I wanted it to stop. I wanted to go to her. I wanted to hold her in my arms. I wanted to wake from this nightmare and for life to be normal. Panic rose in my throat when I realised I had a new normal and empty life. No more twirling skirts or dolly games. No fancy dancing or back seat singing. No pretty shoes or plastic beads. No little girl with big brown eyes to bring cuddles and kisses in the early morning. No Crystal. Little girls didn't live here anymore. This was my new normal life and I hated it.

I stood still for the next six months while the world rushed by. Outside sounds of life penetrated my black bubble but the words were incoherent. I was numb and the pain I felt would only ease with alcohol, which had become my constant companion.

But then the light began to seep into my prison and I felt the stirrings of life in my heart. The dark nights and lonely days had stirred questions and I needed answers. I enrolled in a community based childcare course to help alleviate my guilt. I was sure I had been an inept mother and needed outside reassurance I had done the right thing. I received the highest recorded score. I bought a set of tarot cards to seek answers and became quite a hit amongst my friends for my accurate readings, although I did not find my daughter there.

Eventually I joined the gym. Exercise can unblock grief in a positive manner. When you grieve, it causes blockages in your natural energy flow. Getting the energy to circulate again can be a relevant factor in the healing process. Just a simple twenty-minute walk will do wonders to prevent any negative grief energy from stagnating. This energy can become quite dense and lead to even more depression. After Martin passed away, my mother had taken up pushbike riding with amazing results. It was only at this time that I started to follow her advice.

The seasons changed, the wind blew, the rain fell and another year rolled to an end. Slowly, I began to smile again and then I remembered how to laugh. Crystal was my first waking thought and my last thought at night every day. Despite my sadness, the sun began to shine. The following year, I qualified as an aerobics instructor and became pregnant with my first son, Alan. My meaningless existence regained meaning and the light, twice extinguished, was relit. Crystal still lived in my heart and echoed in my mind, but my newborn son was the medicine I needed to heal my scarred and broken life.

Alan's dad and I endured a fiery relationship, peppered with arguments and seasoned with alcohol and drugs. We both worked hard, saved our money, partied all weekend and in 1994, five years after Alan, our second son, Jack, burst into the world.

At that time, we lived in a small town and the cracks were widening in our relationship. Three more summers kissed the end of our relationship goodbye. I truly loved the boys' father and tried my best for the twelve years we lasted. When alcohol and drugs line the family nest, problems always prevail.

I was hard hit and immediately coupled with another alcoholic. The lessons from the past rose again, this time harder and uglier than before. Drinking was making me sick, so I found a new addiction, the amphetamine Speed. I only took a little over twelve months to hit rock bottom with this new drug, my boys by my side. I tried to hold onto them but my selfishness had become too strong. The drug was the only thing that mattered.

My dad passed away early in 1999. Five months later, the family court and the boys' father justifiably declared me an unfit mother. The boys were removed from my care. Once again, I sank into a black sea of depression, but this time my companion was a dangerous drug: amphetamines.

I spun a cocoon of shame, guilt and sorrow around me and hid myself from the world. I stood precariously on the edge of insanity when the voices began to whisper. Thirteen years after her death, I heard my daughter's voice: "Mummy, mummy your life is in danger!"

The other voices were my spirit family who had had enough of watching my mother cry. She had lost so much, first her son, then her beloved granddaughter and now it seemed her daughter was lost as well.

I stirred in my cocoon. Day in and day out, I listened to the voices who berated me, counselled me, loved me and finally convinced me to stop the drugs and regain my life as a much missed mother and daughter.

When spirit has a will, spirit has a way. After two years, I stopped the drugs.

When the four seasons cycled again, I emerged as a strong, determined and passionate medium.

Chapter 1

Iboarded the plane and settled in my seat. The plane taxied across the runway and lifted into the sky. As we flew high above the earth and over fat lazy white clouds, I reflected on my life as a medium.

Most people believe mediums are bombarded by the spirit world 24/7. This would be a fair statement for some newly awakened mediums who often find their new abilities frightening and confusing, but was no longer true for me. As your gift develops, you soon learn to turn it 'on and off' at will, and that's when the work takes on a whole new meaning.

Once you are able to embrace your new life, a partnership with your spirit guide is formed, and together you push forward to help a grieving world heal.

There is a saying that all mediums are psychic but not all psychics are mediums. This is true, although most mediums prefer to steer away from future predictions and life counselling.

To reunite spirit with the living, try to make sense of a senseless death and teach those who have suffered a loss to recognise the signs and synchronicities the spirit world sends on a daily basis becomes far more important than simply getting a name right or describing a future lover.

My personal passion is to reunite bereaved parents with their spirit children. I have felt this way since the day I knew I possessed this gift.

I began working as a medium in late 2002. I worked hard at perfecting my skills and by early 2004 was working full-time in my new profession. My efforts were recognised by the Australian

Psychics Association and I was awarded Australian Psychic of the Year in 2005.

This award had brought publicity from all corners of the media and I was now on a flight to Melbourne to shoot a segment with a national current affairs program.

I was naturally apprehensive, as this type of program needs to cover both sides of the fence in regard to psychics —the believers and the sceptics. It was the sceptic viewpoint that worried me. I had agreed to conduct a demonstration of my ability to a small studio audience.

I had confidence in my ability, although having already participated in this type of program in 2004, I knew how nervous I could become and also how it may affect the process.

My youngest son, Jack, had accompanied me on this trip and his natural excitement at being on a plane for the first time and also the luxury of a posh hotel helped to steady my nerves.

The shooting of the segment took more than a day. When it was all over, I felt pretty good about it all and totally relieved. The sceptical reporter had come down hard on me, however, I had turned a room of fence sitters into believers, so I knew it would be a fairly good outcome.

When the show was broadcast, the reaction was overwhelming. The previous program had only aired in Brisbane. This one was nationwide, and I was little prepared for the tidal wave of requests that bombarded me solidly for the next month.

There were requests from people for all types of things, from future readings to lost cats. Through it all, I kept my head cool and insisted Mandy, my assistant, only made appointments for people who wished to communicate with their loved ones in spirit. Poor Mandy was run off her feet and in the middle of all this chaos, my first tour of the east coast of Australia was born.

My guides had told me the preceding year that I needed to get to the heart of Australia and tour the regional centres. Mandy and I researched and found fifty towns with a population of fifty thousand or more and mapped out a tour.

Touring the regional towns was wise in a business sense. I found it much easier to get attention from the local press in small towns. I had no money to finance a tour so I applied for and got twelve thousand dollars in credit. I organised a very cheap television commercial and spent every dollar I had.

In mid February 2006, I borrowed a further hundred dollars for petrol from my mother and set off on my first Australian tour.

Chapter 2

Mandy and I travelled south for the first leg of the tour. We had eight shows in the first leg and had absolutely no idea how it would all go. Mediums were only just beginning to be accepted in Australia and with my limited budget, advertising was challenging. It was no surprise, but disappointing, to find some shows with only a handful of patrons in the room.

It seemed like everyone and everything was against me. Some venues were allowing other mediums to book in only two or three days prior to my scheduled event. This was heartbreaking as in most cases I had booked the venue months before. Considering how new the concept of psychic shows was in Australia, it was also very surprising.

Each show, nonetheless, seemed to build strength and confidence in my ability. By the time I arrived at the second last venue, I was determined to let nothing stop me from doing the work I felt was so badly needed: giving proof that the afterlife existed. Each show brought some amazing moments. One in particular stands out in my memory, with a man who a few short weeks before would never have contemplated sitting in such an audience. He was a hard-core sceptic.

His name was Alex. His son, Paul, had passed away only three weeks before my show. He was a young man when he died unexpectedly due to a misdiagnosed heart condition.

It is little surprise to me that many people like Alex, are sceptical of the work I do. It challenges deep-seated beliefs dating back to the beginning of time. In addition, many in this field aren't as ethical as they could be. There has been a lot of publicity about charlatans but not a great deal about the positive aspects of this work.

It all comes back to not understanding exactly how mediums work. There are very few open-minded investigators conducting scientific studies into psychic abilities, and when they present their findings to their peers, their work is often rejected as not having enough objective information.

Alex happened to be sitting about halfway to the back in a somewhat negative but slightly hopeful frame of mind. He felt I was a phony and was only there to prove a point to his daughter. His family, who lived far and wide, was grief-stricken, especially once they found out that the death could have been avoided. Alex was suffering greatly.

His second wife, Marie, read about my upcoming show at a venue only five minutes from their house and Alex's daughter, Julie, wanted to go as she had a strong belief in the afterlife.

Alex initially refused to go because of his scepticism, but eventually relented when he saw how upset Julie was.

In spite of the large crowd at the show that night, Alex and Julie received a reading. Alex later told me that he was amazed at the messages that came out that night. He could not believe that I could get so much right. I even got Paul's nickname, Teddy. That night, Alex left a changed man and when the family added up how many points of validation they had received from Paul, it totalled over thirty!

I know that Alex is now reading everything he can lay his hands on regarding spirituality and the afterlife and believes he is a much better person. He is not so angry now that he knows that Paul is only a thought away. I have talked to him and emailed frequently. With each email emerged a much more peaceful man.

In a recent phone call, Alex told me that he tries to meditate regularly and now communicates with Paul in his own way. He even tells others who are grieving how they too can see the signs for themselves. He still misses his son and always will. However, becoming spiritual and understanding that death is a doorway to the next dimension has lifted this lovely man to a new level of personal contentment.

Alex just reaffirms my belief that although it is great to receive initial confirmation from a medium, the spirit world would like family members and friends to feel free to talk to them and know they are there. It is good for the souls of us who are left behind to know we travel with spirit.

I feel it is important to be open but remaining a little sceptical is healthy. However, if you are receiving a reading, try to let your guard down as scepticism can cause a block in the process and make it very hard to receive information.

I remember a sceptic at an earlier show who really only came to have a bit of fun and keep her friends company. The group she went with were all drinking and were quite rowdy. On the rare occasion that this happens, I just ignore the drinkers. But on this particular night, one spirit decided to turn them around. I went to a blond woman in the group and told her I had a father figure in spirit for her. With her arms crossed, she agreed that her father was in spirit. I gave a few validations. She kept nodding but I could see that she was having none of it. That was when I saw her dad hold a little handmade ashtray in the palm of his hand. I received the impression she still had it. As I relayed the message, her whole face changed and tears began to roll down her face.

After the show, she admitted that she had thought I was bogus until her dad came through. With tears in her eyes, she told me that the only thing she had been given was a small ashtray that her father had made himself and that absolutely no one knew that. I do believe that her dad taught her a lesson that night and I am glad to say it was a good one.

Something that is quite common in the shows is psychic amnesia, when an audience member is put on the spot and forgets all relatives except the one they really want to contact. When this happens, it can actually take down the energy of the whole show and may make sceptics even firmer in their beliefs.

After the first leg of the tour, I only had two days off. We then headed to the regional towns of western NSW with my new travelling assistant in tow. Mandy had a family and was needed at home as well as in my office, to cope with the ever-increasing demands for my work.

Once again I found other psychics trying to muscle in on my venues. At one venue in particular, I was faced with a crowd that seemed quite put out by my presence.

Apparently, a medium who was much better known had cancelled only a few days before my event and some, who obviously felt I would not deliver as well as her, decided to purchase tickets for my event.

It made me feel very bad but I meditated myself into happiness before I started. When I walked on stage, I tried to lighten the atmosphere by cracking a joke, which seemed to further sink my ship. They truly did not want to be there.

My guides told me to ignore them and directed me to a serene looking woman in the third row. When I first tuned into this elegant woman, I had no idea her serene face hid one of the biggest nightmares a woman can face. Her name was Deanne.

Chapter 3

Deanne was only 18 when she gave birth to a stillborn son. In the year following this tragic occurrence, her father died. Her mum passed away with Alzheimer's nine years later, being diagnosed with the disease only two weeks after the death of her father. In essence, she lost both her parents in a short period of time.

With one son, Curt, holding her hand, she started a new life with her second husband, John. Before long, she gave birth to another son, Jackson, followed three years later with a daughter, Jasmine.

Two weeks before Christmas of 2005, Jackson had taken the day off school due to an allergic reaction in his eye and went on a run with John in his cattle truck. Deanne spoke to her two boys at 3.30pm to see how they were enjoying their day. All was well in her world and before she hung up, she told her son that she loved him.

Deanne was an accomplished pianist and on that fine night in December was playing at a Christmas function with a jazz trio. At 7.50pm that night as Deanne slid her fingers over the ivories and music swam around her, a truck laden with cattle lost control on a bend and exploded on impact. Both occupants of the truck were killed instantly. It was Jackson and John.

Deanne had no idea that an accident had occurred and when she returned home went straight to bed. It was not until 12.30am the next morning when awoken by a knock at the door by the police that Deanne learned her life had changed forever. Everything began to move in slow motion as the reality sunk in. Her rock and her Angel were gone.

As the world stopped spinning and her heart exploded, she was well aware of the journey that lay ahead; this was a road she knew too well. Deanne somehow found the strength to stand tall for her daughter and make the necessary call to her son, Curt. On the outside she was a tower of strength, but on the inside she only wished to lie down and never wake up again. Deanne had travelled this road before but it had not been so rough, nor had it been so unrelenting, and as much as she wished it away, there were no exits.

Deanne possessed a firm belief in the afterlife and knew that John was aware of this. It had only been three months since that tragic day when she booked a ticket for my show. She knew in her heart that if there was a way for John to get through, he would.

I will never forget the night I met Deanne. Looking at her, you would never have known what she had just been faced with. Her mother came first, followed by her dad and then they showed me seashells. It was then that Jackson came up to me and told me he was her son. I knew he was young and I knew that he had died in an accident.

As I relayed the information, I felt another spirit come forward who told me he was the little boy's father. Then they told me they had died in the same accident, I had to hold my emotion back.

The father was the strongest of the two spirits and told me that their names started with J. He also told me the other family members' names. He told me he was a truck driver and that he had been driving on that fateful night only a few months earlier. He showed himself as a tall man with a big head and dark hair. Detail after detail was relayed and I could see Deanne melting with each validation.

She later told me that watching me talk to her boys confirmed her belief that they lived on and gave her more peace and strength than she could ever have hoped for. She told me the reading gave her two weeks break from deep grief. It was a very powerful connection that embraced the core of my own soul with compassion and empathy. Deanne and I met many more times and her boys became as familiar to me as my own family.

Months later, I invited Deanne to a healing seminar I was holding and she travelled six hours on a bus to attend. After the seminar, I gave Deanne a lift back to her motel where we had a coffee and discussed the day. After about half an hour, I saw a face start to swim before my eyes. It was a young boy with strawberry blonde hair and a shy smile who was going to great effort to show me the lizard he had just found.

He was so sweet in nature and I knew I had just seen Jackson for the first time. In previous readings he stood back and let his dad do the talking, but finally he was there giving his mum messages.

I am not sure how Deanne felt that day, but I felt that a barrier had been broken. As much as Deanne was accepting her husband's death, she had been stuck on Jackson's. I knew when I left Deanne that day that she still had a long and painful road to travel. But in my heart, I felt this brave woman would do great things with her life and that her pain would eventually help many.

Ironically, the town we held the seminar in was also playing host to another event that weekend: 'Lights on the Hill'. This is a gathering of people who get together to honour truck drivers killed on the road. I smiled when I realised the trouble her family had gone to in order to help her heal and the love I felt shining on Deanne was a tonic to my soul.

Deanne and I have had many conversations on the phone since that time and she increasingly grows in strength. She told me on numerous occasions that she understood everything I was relaying in the seminar, and had long held the belief that we reincarnate and choose our current lives prior to birth.

She also confessed that while I lectured at the seminar, she felt like she already knew what I was saying. Nothing was a surprise. It was as though the information was etched in her soul. She understands that all the grief and pain she has experienced is a part of her soul contract and knowing that she willingly agreed to this life is what makes her strong. She is one of the most inspirational women I have ever met.

While we travel our physical life, our souls are travelling a spiritual journey. Both our soul and our physical incarnation have goals. The physical goal is well known to us and can include having children, buying a house, travelling the world or simply running a successful business. During the course of a lifetime, many events occur to prevent us from attaining these goals. More often than not, we blame our misfortune on bad luck or we push the blame to another person. When someone dies, we blame God or in the case of a road accident, we blame the other vehicle. In the case of single vehicle accidents, I have had people beg me to give them some kind of explanation in the hope they'll have someone to blame.

We refuse to accept our fate and constantly look externally to lay the blame. We find acceptance and forgiveness bitter pills to swallow. Judgement, revenge and other low vibrational emotions are far easier to digest.

Everyone has a soul that lives for eternity. Our soul will have many lives and each life, we will incarnate in a body and pick a set of living circumstances that will best serve our needs to attain our common goal of perfection. In simple words, our soul strives to be as wise and as all-knowing as the creator and then returns to the source from which we were created.

Eventually we will attain such a high level of skills and wisdom that we will cease to incarnate and will choose to assist other incarnating souls in reaching higher levels.

We are all on different learning levels in both our physical and soul journey. It would be ludicrous to place a grade one student in university as it would to allow a lower level soul to live the life of an advanced one.

Deanne is surviving her tragic life circumstances simply because she has incarnated with the right amount of knowledge to overcome her plight. She could have been eaten up with grief, rendered incoherent with alcohol and depression. This would have had an adverse effect on her young daughter and son, but instead she has risen up and is not only a wonderful mother but also an inspiration to the many that cross her path. She is teaching by example.

The soul will not choose a life it is not prepared for. The strength to overcome whatever hardship we face is within each of us. We only need to make the right choices and utilise the appropriate opportunities to survive any tragedy. If we do not choose correctly and remain angry and bitter about our lives, we will ultimately return to the spirit realms with unfinished lessons.

This will be a source of frustration for our soul, and another life will have to be lived to attain the chosen goal. If we do rise to the challenge of each lesson offered, we will find when we return to the spirit realms, that our soul has advanced and the lessons faced in this life will not have to be endured again.

Deanne showed me a quality I had rarely seen: Grace. She showed me how to stay dignified in the face of total destruction. She inspired me to teach others how to achieve this seemingly unattainable state on the often tragic road of life.

This tour of regional Australia was teaching me great things. I was meeting people who had faced the most horrific circumstances and survived. They were creeping into my heart and staying there. Spirit children were coming thick and fast. The more bereaved parents I met, the more determined I was to help and educate them. There were so many misinformed people. My guides kept directing me to people who would cause me to think and from whom I would learn. My soul also knew secrets, and with each passing mile, they were being unlocked.

Chapter 4

In March 2006, I self-published my first book *Spirit Whispers*. I was excited about the release yet also a little fearful of the reception it would receive. It had been hard to be honest but I have long found honesty to be the best way to go. It would be terrible to have someone else be honest for you. Their version might be a little more colourful than the truth.

I need not have worried as those who did read it wrote long emails about how much they loved it. My mum read her copy many times, as did a lot of other people.

Self-publishing is a harder road to travel in the world of books and I found book reviewers were not beating my door down to get a copy, let alone read the many free copies I sent out. Reviews were out of the question. I sold quite a few copies at my shows and some of the New Age shops agreed to stock them.

It seemed that I still had a long way to go. Despite my newfound skills at acquiring free press, the shows were not exactly bursting at the seams. Money was an ever-growing concern and my original debt had increased by quite a few thousand dollars, but I pressed on.

The shows were addictive. The smiles and validations after successful readings were fuelling the machine I had built. Behind the scenes, Mandy was getting more and more readings booked in. Word was spreading and my book *Spirit Whispers* was also encouraging people to give me a try. Average Australians were finding that they could identify with the story of my life and were keen to open up to see if their grief could be healed.

One woman took a brave step forward. Her name is Sharon.

In January 2006, Sharon had a distressing conversation with her son Adam. He wanted her to know what he wished for at his own funeral. He insisted but the woman argued she wanted no part in such a sinister conversation. Twenty years earlier, she was driving with her two-year-old son, Matthew, when a car coming out of an intersection hit hers on the passenger side. So horrific was the accident that her car wrapped itself like a metal boomerang around the front of the other driver's car. Her two year old did not survive but somehow Sharon did. There were no goodbyes and there was no closure. As Sharon lay in a hospital bed unable to move, they buried her first-born son.

She left her partner and father of her two other children four years later and struggled on as a single mother despite her grief, which she buried deep within her soul. When her father passed away, an unbreakable bond formed between Sharon, her two children, Christy and Adam, her mother and her sister Dawn. Then, with young Tara being born in 1996, the family of six was complete.

Adam became the man of this strongly feminine family at only eleven years of age and all of his women adored him. It was little wonder with Sharon's past history that she did not want her son to talk so openly about his own death. She insisted she would be the first to go and would never have a need for what she considered useless information. Adam, however, would not stop until she listened. He told her what he wanted to happen at his funeral right down to the music and coffin bearers. Sharon agreed to listen just to stop him talking in such a manner and Adam seemed happy he had told her his plans. Little did she know that only three days later, she would remember this conversation.

Sharon had taken a friend to visit an aunt about 80kms away when she received a phone call from Adam's girlfriend Lisa. She was hysterical as she relayed to Sharon that Adam had been hit by a car on his motorbike and was not moving.

The afternoon passed as a confusing nightmare with Sharon becoming almost psychotic and her emotions running out of control. She was sure that Lisa was wrong, that somehow Adam only had a few broken bones. However, the next morning she was faced with the task of identifying her beautiful son at the morgue.

As she viewed her son on the stainless steel slab in the clinical coldness of an empty room, she noticed a single tear drop from the corner of his eye. It moved down the side of his face in slow motion, disappearing into his hairline. Sharon knew that this was the last tear her son would ever shed. In that one moment, her heart shattered into a million pieces.

Sharon shut out all who remained in her life; her only wish was to be with her son wherever that may be.

Three months later, I was waiting for my next client when I felt a young male spirit come into my reading room. I opened the door to a woman and her daughter. This was a little confusing because my booking list told me that I had two friends arriving to be read separately. They explained that the friend was sick and that Lisa, the daughter, had come to take her place. I said that I preferred to read family members together and ushered them into the room.

That was the first time I met Adam.

He showed me exactly how he had died in full colour. I could see the bike with the car hitting him. He wanted me to say 'Happy Birthday' to his mum, Sharon, which was that day and to tell her he was with his brother Matthew. He told me he was great at karaoke. He liked to party with all types of substances and claimed he loved the tattoos everyone had in his honour. He showed me his big beautiful eyes and was very flirty in his nature. He had special messages for his sisters and his mate James. He told me he was responsible for the other woman not coming so Lisa could come instead.

He really needed to connect with his family and saw this as his only chance. Somehow, he synchronised the other lady getting a phone call saying she was needed for work. When spirit wants to connect they will find a way. It will never be harmful, however they pull out no stops to make things happen. I am unsure how they do this, just that they do.

Adam's spirit and presence felt as if he was in flesh that day. He told me he wanted to help his mum and his loved ones understand their loss. He has kept his word.

Chapter 5

I didn't meet Sharon until May 2006 at a demonstration at the local mall. I looked up and saw a forlorn woman standing on her own with a yellow rose in her hand. I immediately felt Adam by my side. He told me that that was his mum.

After the demo, I walked straight up to her and said hello. I told her that Adam was with us, and when she handed me the yellow rose, I asked her how she knew that it was my favourite rose. She told me she had been sitting all alone when a voice told her to buy me a yellow rose and bring it to the mall.

She had heard the tape of the reading I had conducted for Lisa, and as the tears poured from her eyes I could see a woman in big trouble. I felt Adam push at me to do more, so I offered to go to her mum's house and do a reading. Sharon's mum had lung cancer and could not get around easily. I found out more about young Matthew the day I went to Sharon's mum's house and it was clear to me that Sharon was not just grieving for Adam, but that all the buried grief she had for Matthew was coming to the surface. She was pushing away her remaining children and every time I called her, all she could do was cry. She was totally inconsolable.

I felt it would be great to get her to a healing seminar and talked her into attending the next one. On the day of the seminar, I could see Sharon getting stuck on forgiveness and by the end of the day was unsure if it had been of any help at all.

I did not call her for a while as I was busy with shows but I did worry about her. I noticed that her posts on my website forum were becoming more positive, but with no communication I was unprepared for the change when I finally did speak with her.

It was the day her mum passed from lung cancer. I was very worried for this woman had endured so much pain. Two major deaths in eleven months was a lot to bear. I called her as soon as I heard, and nearly dropped the phone when I realised she was not only okay but totally together despite the sadness of the day. I listened in disbelief as she relayed the events following the seminar. Sharon had never seen a sign from her son but when she got in the car to leave the seminar, she turned on the radio. She could barely believe it when the following four songs were Adam's favourites.

She cried tears of joy all the way home and realised that it *was* Adam who wanted her to stop being sad. If she could just do that, he would be able to show her signs all the time. She finally understood that Adam was exactly where he was meant to be and that she still had her sons, just not in a physical body. She thanked me again for the seminar and relayed all the signs she had received since that day.

Her mum had passed away but she no longer feared death and knew without a doubt that her loved ones were with her. It was the most amazing transformation I had ever seen and I thanked my guides for helping me develop the seminar.

Recently, Sharon was helping me with an experiment and Adam was in his spot, on the arm of my chair. When it was time to leave, he pulled a cigarette from behind his ear, asked me to tell the 'old girl' it was time to go and then bent and gave me a kiss on the cheek. "Thanks for helping the old girl," he said. I relayed his actions to Sharon and we both cried. Sharon then told me that they had put a cigarette behind his ear in the coffin and that Adam always called her 'old girl.'

Despite her grief over his death, Sharon had never doubted that Adam's time was up. His conversation only three days prior confirmed it. She has told me it was comforting to know exactly what he wanted done at his funeral and an honour to respect his wishes.

When my daughter died, the dream I had two days previously confirmed it was her time. When my brother passed away, my mother had a premonition and insisted on showing me her will a week prior to the event.

There was a recent article in the paper about a young girl who complained to her mother of terrifying dreams in which an old woman would come out of a tent and tell her she was going to die. She was murdered three months later.

I have countless stories of signs received before a tragedy. In most cases, the victim will talk about their own funerals and what they would like done. There can be a sense of foreboding with family members, who often dream about the event beforehand.

I am certain that the spirit world sends us these signs to prepare us for the upcoming event. When the major grief has passed, the sign can be a useful tool in helping us understand that the death was timely. In my own experience, it has helped immensely. I have known since the day my daughter passed that it wouldn't have mattered where she was. Whether in a car, on a boat or even in a pool, she would have passed away on the day she did. The spirit world made that clear two days prior to her death.

It is apparent to me that we all have a time when we will return to the spirit realms. However, the truth is the soul is eternal and although our physical body dies, our soul does not. There truly is no reason to say goodbye, as we will meet the people we love and honour again and undoubtedly live further lives with them. Each life will be chosen to balance any past life karma, and as souls, we all advance on different levels.

Think of life as a movie where all the actors work so well together that they choose to work in other movies again. The movies are our lives, the actors our friends and family.

In each town I passed through, I was confronted with many new revelations and even more confusion. The problem was that there were too many different views of the spirit world by too many ego-driven practitioners.

This was creating fear in the newly awakened Australian public. The questions at each show began revolving around the topic of evil spirits. There were dark tales of objects being thrown across rooms, but when I questioned whether anyone else had witnessed such happenings, the answer was always negative. Others had been told to protect themselves from the unthinkable.

It bugged me. It still does. I remember the days when the spirit world was not apparent to me and rarely discussed. My social group back then never talked about chairs and objects being mysteriously flung across the room. Now, however, I was being confronted with these amazing tales of invalidated fantasy.

One of the recurrent questions is always about heaven and hell. I have discussed this at length with my guides and others I respect in the business. Most of us agree that hell is a state of mind.

Chapter 6

We are all spirits having a human experience. We have all incarnated many times before this life. Sometimes we are males and other times we are female. We set out in each life with a set of lessons or goals we wish to achieve. These goals generally work toward the greater good of mankind.

We learn from love and we learn from fear. For instance, our mother may be a nurturing person we can always depend upon to bring us reassurance, comfort and love. Our father may be a harsh and unforgiving man who may strike fear in us from our earliest memories. From our mother we learn love and compassion, from our father we can learn how NOT to treat our children, or we can allow our fear of him to distort our minds. If we do suffer a life with a harsh parent, the lesson is there to learn. Some will become amazing parents; adamant that they will not be the parent their father was. Others will follow their father's footsteps and also become harsh and unforgiving. In this case, the soul would have failed the planned lesson. It is important to understand that we learn from tensions of the opposites, negative and positive.

To achieve our goals of perfection, most souls prefer to use planet Earth as a training ground or school. Earth is a place of great beauty and joy, but also harbours ignorance, hate and suffering that are man-made; not to mention natural planetary disasters over which we have little control. Earth is a perfect testing ground for souls wishing to learn the lessons of forgiveness, judgement, unconditional love and acceptance, thereby developing at a personal soul level. However, many trappings can lure people and sway them from their chosen path. Greed, power, jealousy and lust can become responsible for endless sins and crimes against our fellow humans. Eventually, all human beings will die and their souls will return to spirit.

I am quite often asked about evil spirits and how I protect myself from them. I do not use any form of protection whatsoever. I have very strong guides, and I have always felt protected by them without having to cover myself with white light or whatever else. In my mind, you only protect yourself if you have something to fear and I simply have nothing to fear.

One question that keeps emerging since I began my journey as a medium is what happens to evil people on Earth. Do they go to hell? Do they become evil spirits? More and more I am dealing with people who think they have an evil spirit in their house. With the emergence of the new age world, many charlatans are cashing in on this fear, and charging excessive amounts of money to rid their fearful clients of the 'evil' spirit. This makes my blood boil.

First and foremost, I feel that hell is a state of mind, and feel it mainly resides right here on Earth. I am sure that people who die and have done some bad things on Earth would spend a certain amount of time in life review. They might have to redeem themselves somehow. During a reading I did for a woman, her father came through and admitted he had sexually abused his daughter for many years. I was not quite sure if I should relay what I had heard. He urged me to, saying he needed her to know how sorry he felt. When I did, she told me it was true and tears rushed down her face as she once again relived her childhood horrors.

He later told me what he had done was inexcusable, and that he was trying hard to make up for the damage he had caused and wanted to know if there was a chance his child would forgive him. She told me that she would. The knowledge that he was finally admitting it and understanding how wrong it had been went a long way. This man was what some would classify as evil. When his physical body dropped away, he was forced to review his life and to face the consequences of his actions. His soul was harbouring shame and he only wished to apologise and beg forgiveness.

I presume that facing up to his actions would have been a self-imposed prison for a while, but I feel that his understanding and forgiving daughter gave him the key to the door. In this reading, I could see clearly that this father had taught his daughter one of the most important lessons: the lesson of forgiveness. Not only did she free herself but also the soul of her misguided father. During the reading I felt nothing evil about this man, I only felt a spirit that needed to make things right.

Evil is a word I do not like much because I do not see people as evil but only as 'away from the light'. I prefer to call evil darkness. Throughout our lives, there will be times where we move away from the light for short or long periods of time. It is part of our life journey to get back on the path and travel once again toward the light. Some people never will and when they die, I do NOT believe that they become dark spirits waiting to prey on innocent minds and souls. This type of thinking belongs in horror stories. I do not believe that they can physically hurt us nor do I believe that they want to.

You see, all the things that make people bad or dark happen on the physical plane and belong to this realm. Those who indulge in drugs and alcohol may be perceived as bad on Earth, but when you take away the addictive substances that made them that way, they can no longer perform acts that may be interpreted as bad. Some people go so far as to say that the spirit world gets into the energy field of the substance abusers on Earth and makes them do evil things. I totally disagree with this way of thinking and although I know it has been written in books long ago, I feel it is time that we updated our beliefs. When you next find yourself reading something that was written a long time ago, consider human evolution and ask yourself if it is still true.

When I first began to notice the spirit world, spirits were negative to me; they taunted me and were quite cruel. However, when I look back I can clearly see they were reflecting my own self-hatred back at me and all the taunts were to get me back to the light. Believe me when I say that it is hard to stay in the dark for too long if you are a child of the light. When you constantly think badly about yourself and feel stuck in a dark place, you may very well blame the spirit world for making your life miserable. It is rather that what you are putting out to the universe is coming back to you tenfold.

In all the readings I have conducted, I have never found a single evil spirit. It has been suggested that my guides have spared me from this, but I beg to differ. Why would my guides, who threw all my own negative feelings back at me in the dark days, spare me from anything? I truly believe that evil belongs to this world. Money can bring about darkness, as can sex and drug abuse. All of these things happen on the physical plane not in the spirit realm. Killing or torturing someone is a physical act that, once again, cannot be performed in a non-physical reality.

Remember that we are spirits having a human experience, and if indeed there has to be a positive and negative to everything, then perhaps it is wise to consider that we are spirits living in the physical, negative realm with all our insecurities, physical ailments and misunderstandings. Living on Earth is not easy, and this is completely understood by our guides and teachers in the realms. No matter who we were on Earth or what we did, each one of us will be accepted equally when we die.

Another common misconception brought about by television shows and compounded by some mediums is the idea that spirits need to be shown the way to the light.

I cannot understand this way of thinking. With all the enlightened beings in the universe, why would a spirit need to be shown the way home by an earthbound human who has limited or little remembered knowledge of the spirit world?

If you asked me what the spirit world was like, I would truthfully answer that I don't know or don't remember. I sense that it is a wonderful place and perhaps our soul life is our true life; this life being merely a weekend away from it. I am however not certain. In my soul I feel I have lived many lives, but only get flashes here and there. I am not convinced that psychics of any kind definitively have the ability to tune into a person's past lives.

It truly bugs me when psychics and mediums profess to know for sure, and claim they have the ability to guide the dead to the light. It is not fair to people who are suffering grief, and once again, creates an unnecessary fear.

Chapter 7

One morning at the end of October 2005, a heavy fog had descended on the highway near where I lived. It was pea soup thick and most of the traffic had slowed down to compensate for the low visibility. At 5.15am, a young man was driving to work and at 5.19am, came to an intersection only 2kms away from where I lay peacefully sleeping. He checked the traffic on the highway and drove off when he thought it was all clear. Out of the fog, a semi trailer came hurtling toward him and slammed into his car with such impact that he was pushed onto the middle traffic island, all the panels on the driver's side being completely torn off his car. This young man's name was Daniel.

A car arrived on the scene shortly afterwards, followed five minutes later by another one. The driver of the second car was Daniel's sister, Annette. She was beside herself, as you could imagine, and frantically called her mother. He was still alive at this point and she desperately waited for the ambulance to arrive. Daniel was no ordinary boy. He was a survivor who had battled leukaemia his whole life, cheating death time and again. His family had stood by his side patiently as he lay in hospital beds receiving transfusions. As the youngest and only boy, he was held in high regard by his parents and three sisters.

He was transported to hospital and sadly passed away at 7.20am.

At 8.40am, I was unaware of the accident and was quite shocked when I discovered it shortly after leaving home. It was total chaos and as I drove past Daniel's car, I knew that a young man had died that day. I knew this with certainty because he jumped in my car and started to ask questions. I could not hold the emotion back as he cried and asked me what he should do. He looked at his car and kept saying, "Oh no, what has happened? What about my family? Look at my car!" He begged me for help but I could do nothing but cry with him. I explained to him that his family would survive somehow and that everything would work out. I was so upset at his grief that I cried uncontrollably on and off for the entire day. I thought of him daily and wondered how his family were. As the days passed, flowers kept appearing at the accident site and every day I had to check my emotion.

Thirteen days later, we met again. I was conducting a reading for a woman whose own son had passed due to leukaemia when I saw the accident site in a vision. I asked my client if she knew of a young man that had passed with a D name very recently. He gave me the name Daniel. He was the same young man I had encountered at the accident site. I then told my client exactly where and how he had passed and asked if she could please get a message to his family. Every day after that, I would hear the song 'Daniel' by Elton John as I passed the site…

In February 2006, a magazine contacted me and told me that they were going to run the story I had submitted 14 months previously. You may not find this strange, but it is when you think of a psychic medium submitting a story to a motorbike magazine called 'Oz Bike' which supports the bikers' way of life in Australia. I had only sent the story on a whim and did not expect them to reply and was more than a little surprised when they did. Unknown to me at that time was that Daniel was also an avid 'Oz Bike' reader. The article came out in March and his family bought the issue to honour Daniel's memory. Annette called me immediately after she read the article and expressed her surprise at such an article in a magazine usually dominated by tattoos, bikes and breasts. We arranged a date for a reading and on Daniel's 21st birthday, we met again.

As soon as the family sat down I started to connect and it was not long before I once again recognised the accident site. I turned to the family and said, "this is Daniel and he died fairly recently!"

They were very surprised that I knew him and I explained how I had met him. I sat with the family for two hours - such was their grief. All the while, Daniel was giving validations. He whistled the start of 'Patience' by Guns and Roses, which brought on laughter as it was one he was always trying to perfect. He told me about his sister's tattoo and explained that his mum had a tiki in her pocket that belonged to him. He told me how Annette had fixed his hair for him, and mostly he told them he was okay. As they were walking out the door, I told them how I always heard the Elton John song 'Daniel' as I drove past his accident site and they told me that they played that song at his funeral. I have kept in close contact with the family since that day, and quite often get calls from them all on the same day. The family is definitely dealing with the pain. Despite the fact that Annette was the first on the scene, she now seems to be a lot more accepting.

Daniel is very dear to me and has proved that in the case of accidents, spirits go through a period of disorientation. I feel that they rush up to people asking what has happened, and in this case Daniel found a medium. However, not for a minute did I feel I needed to send him anywhere or help him in any way. I knew he would receive the assistance he required before long. I also felt strongly that he had to go through this after-death orientation to condition him to his new dimension.

I passed another site recently where an accident had just occurred, and the same thing happened. As I passed by, I could not tell what had happened as there was only one vehicle present. Next, I heard a voice tell me it was a bike accident. I couldn't however see the bike. In a flash, a man in his late twenties or early thirties jumped in my car in spirit form. I asked him his name and thought he said Greg. He asked me what had happened and I told him he had an accident and that he was now in spirit. I was running late for my regular Chi-Gung class and I told him he would be okay. On the way back, there was still activity around the accident site. It was then that I saw the bike, wedged firmly under a four-wheel drive. The spirit jumped back in my car again. He asked me why it happened and I explained that it was his time. I told him that someone would come for him soon and then he was gone. A few days later, I found out that his name was Craig not Greg and I realised once again that this young man was in the stage of adapting to his new space the very moment I drove past.

Another incident of immediate communication was with Uncle Arthur. I was doing a reading for his niece and she was there to connect to her dad, William. During the course of the reading, William told me that Uncle Arthur had just turned up. The woman told me she had no Uncle Arthur in spirit, so I let it go. All day during every reading, a quiet little voice would tell me that his name was Arthur and I would ask the client in front of me if this made sense. No one claimed him, so he just sat quietly and waited. After work that day, I received a call from the first lady who was there for William and she told me that her Uncle Arthur had died during the reading. Poor old uncle Arthur! I cannot imagine what he must have thought being stuck in a medium's office all day wondering if this was indeed the pearly gates.

Through all the readings I have conducted, it has become apparent that spirits can communicate with a medium immediately after passing away. However, I do not think that it is a great idea to seek out this type of validation directly after a death. This has more to do with honouring the grieving period, and I have found that a reading will be smoother if the client has come to some sort of acceptance.

If a reading is sought too soon, it is clear that emotion and grief will block the process and the reading will not be as clear as it could be. So please know that your spirits are able to communicate, but do give *yourself* time before you rush out and see a medium. It is far better to remain open to the signs the spirit is sending you and to wait approximately six months to make an appointment.

Chapter 8

It was the end of April 2006 and I had already visited thirty-five towns. I was tired and broke. The numbers were not going so well and we were stuck in a motel waiting for the night of the show. I had driven seven hundred kilometres to get to the town. I was also as sick as a dog, having picked up a bug somewhere.

The strangest thing happened in that town. We had two days to wait before we could do the show. I stayed in bed the whole time as I could not breathe or even think straight. The morning of the show I was worried as my head felt so thick and, as it turned out, the spirit world also had concerns.

The night before the show, Mandy had a dream. In the dream, she was at her house with four of her family members and a young girl with long blonde hair named Kim. The house caught on fire and Mandy began to panic. However, the young girl, Kim, was by her side. Kim was urging Mandy to get all her daughter's photos. Tash, Mandy's daughter, had passed in a drowning accident so there was a panic, even in the dream, to make sure the photos were safe. After the dream, Mandy lay awake completely puzzled by the strangeness of it all. The morning of the show, she called me and we both wondered what it could mean.

That night, I walked into a room with only fifteen people present. I was so disappointed as I had driven so far and paid so much money to get here. I was now in serious financial trouble and had no idea how I was ever going to recover.

I never allow financial worry to affect my work; so despite my stuffy head, began a most remarkable show. The reading that stood out the most was a young girl named Kim who had died and yes, she had long blonde hair. Mandy's dream was becoming very real.

The young girl had died from illness, so I was still a little puzzled about the meaning of the fire.

Later on, I sold a couple of books and tuned into a woman. I found that she was looking for her nieces and nephews who had passed in a fire. There were four of them, just like in Mandy's dream.

Another strange occurrence at that venue was a resident ghost. When we arrived in the town, we drove to the beautiful old pub where the show was going to take place and were shown the room. I immediately sensed a presence. I am not the type to go ghost hunting, so this was a challenge. I tuned in and felt the spirit had died at the pub and he gave me the name of Arthur. He indicated he had worked there. With no way to absolutely validate that information, I left it at that.

During the next leg of my tour, however, I felt compelled to tell the story at the beginning of my show. A man with long hair put his hand up and told me his grandmother had worked at that pub many years and had told him how the janitor who lived at the pub had died of a heart attack on a bar stool. His name was Arthur. I was pleasantly surprised at this information and it was nice to have it validated.

Working with spirit is different every day and there are many moments that take my breath away. It fills me with awe when I am sought by the spirit world. Not only children seek me this way. Most of the time I can feel spirits come to me a few hours prior to the reading. There have been many occasions before shows when I have felt the presence of a spirit hours before the event, giving me information, almost sitting on my lap, to ensure that their family receive a reading.

Working in a show format is completely different from private readings and takes time to perfect. The energy in the room is a mixture of those from the spirit realms and those in the audience. When you are standing in front of an audience, you are not just confronted with their thoughts and feelings, you are also bombarded with those from the spirit realms.

Spirits are just as anxious to make contact as their living relatives. Their anxiety resembles the Boxing Day sales at Myers! In my mind's eye, I can see the spirits pushing and shoving to be the first to make sure I connect to their loved ones in the audience. I can never be sure exactly how spirits decide who will come forward and who will not, but I suspect the spirit world perceives who will benefit most from a message.

Some spirits are learning how to communicate via a medium. As much as their loved ones wish they would come through, spirits may wait for a future show or private reading. I also suspect that they sometimes wait because their family member in the audience is still too deep in grief to properly accept the messages coming through.

If the spirit is a little nervous, it will affect the clarity of the reading. I have found that when I get a shaky connection with a spirit, it will not be long before another spirit family member will take over the reading and guide the nervous spirit through. My guides also perform this task. Patience pays off. It is also important that spirits know I understand their excitement. I will often say it aloud, and then feel the spirit calm down a little.

I remember once before a reading, a young female spirit rushed into the dressing room and very excitedly told me that her parents would be there. I asked where they might be sitting. She told me exactly which seats and that her name was Kerry. When I went out on stage, I looked to see if there was anyone in those seats, but there wasn't. Then just before I started the readings, a woman took the chair described. I went straight to her and sure enough, she had a daughter in spirit named Kerry.

I shall never forget the elderly spirit lady who had waited a long time to connect with her daughter. She was sending one validation after the other. In my mind's eye I could see her talking away, then she would go into a bedroom and bring out something to show me. This went on for about ten minutes. She was taking a little longer to come back out, so another spirit decided to make a connection.

He had been a farmer in life and very down-to-earth. He was chatting away to his daughter and all of a sudden, I saw the elderly lady return with a box in her hand. The look on her face was priceless, as she demanded to be allowed to talk to her daughter again and tell her about the treasures she had brought out for me to relay. I found it hilarious, especially when she dropped her box and looked unhappily at the farmer who was stepping back. The elderly lady straightened up her dress, picked up her box, gave him a dirty look and back we went to her daughter. It was so funny. I will never forget the look on her face. I do believe she even made my guides wary such was her indignation at having her reading stolen!

When I have these visions, it is like a picture show in my head. I have often burst into laughter when a spirit is describing something to me. They are so funny and always try to lighten the mood of the show. I shall never forget the time this father came through and proudly displayed his ample stomach to me. He even showed me there was a photograph of himself and his heavily pregnant daughter comparing stomachs, which she confirmed.

I nearly choked a little later when another dad came through showing me his beer belly. The first father came back on stage and I was treated to a beer belly competition! As I commentated on what I was seeing, the crowd in the room roared with laughter.

The spirit world is a place where there is a lot of humour and love. Their energy is much lighter as they do not see their deaths as sad, but only as a continuation of their souls' journey. It is clear that they wish their loved ones on Earth to remember the fun times and not to focus on their death. They know we will all meet again and most likely go on to live future lives together. In show readings, they not only prove this point to their loved ones, but also get the message through to the whole audience. This is why shows are so important in medium work.

Chapter 9

How spirit will get my attention never ceases to amaze me. Not to mention the urgency I will feel compelling me to travel for hundreds of kilometres without knowing why.

While planning my next *Spirit Whispers* tour, I was watching the news and viewed a news item about a small country town. As I watched, I felt a warm glow in my heart and felt inspired to look it up to see if it would be worthwhile travelling there. It was.

Leading up to the event, I somehow knew this would be a show to remember, even though there were still some months to go. Every time I saw the name of that town or thought about it, I felt the same warm glow. I was not consciously aware that a young man named Cookie was the spirit calling, and to this day I have never forgotten him.

The afternoon of the show, I felt the young spirit come into the room, or should I say, I saw him. I was listening to my new Pearl Jam CD with headphones when a brilliant blue flash caught my eye. He was a very strong spirit and demanded my immediate attention. I reluctantly took off my headphones and tuned in. I asked for his name and heard Michael but called him Mick. I felt confused and thought this was his name but kept in mind that it might be the person he was looking for. He told me he was killed in a car accident and I sighed; it was sad so many young people died in this manner. He then said 'eighteen' and then 'three.' I asked if he meant 'eighteen years old' and he said no, so I kept the numbers in my mind with an understanding that they would be important. He showed me a black and white scarf, explaining these were the colours of his favourite football team. He told me he was very tall and demonstrated how tall by displaying his energy field to me. I looked up and realised he was well over six foot. He told me that there was another spirit with him. That was the end of the conversation until later.

When we got to the club, I had a feeling this would be a good show as I knew I already had one spirit travelling with me. It was good to go to a show with confidence, especially being for the first time in this town. I have found that in towns where you're unknown, people are generally sceptical until you 'prove' yourself, and this can interfere with the process. My clairaudience is affected most in this case, which I assume is due to the audience sending out ungracious opinions. I think I pick up on their thoughts. At times, it can be difficult to untangle messages from the spirit world and thoughts from the audience. It would be so nice if people could come with an open heart. I know in my heart that the reason is that some mediums who have travelled these towns have left a most unfavourable impression.

This town felt different. I remembered the news article and could still feel the warm glow. When I went into the room, I felt that the energy was good and busy. I knew that more chairs would be needed. When it was time to do my pre-show meditation ritual, I made my way to the curtained area. At 7pm, they began to let the audience in. With just a curtain to block the noise, I had to go and sit in a small storeroom and close the door. It was quite dark but that didn't faze me. It was then that my young visitor chose to speak to me. 'Don', he said or I thought he did, and then he traced a big C initial. I am sure I heard the name Sarah. I just knew his parents were in the audience. I started to feel restless and could hear that more chairs were being brought into the already crowded room. It was going to be a bigger evening than expected. After a quick word to Pete and the other guides present that all was going to be okay, I set off to the room.

You could have heard a pin drop when I entered the room. I poured myself some water into the three waiting glasses. I always start the show with a talk about spirit. I like to explain the whole medium process to relax the audience a bit. I could feel my young spirit urging me to hurry up. I then told the audience about my visitor that afternoon and how keen he was. I decided to start and let this impatient young man through.

I was led directly to a family of three in the front row. I addressed the blonde woman with sad eyes and told her I had a mother figure beside her and I also felt her dad. It was then that they began to 'rock the baby' which is a symbol I use in spirit communication. Basically, it tells me that they have a younger person with them. I realised that this was my young traveller. I explained to the woman that they had a child with them and said that I thought it was hers. She told me that she did have a child in spirit. The woman whispered her answer and I could see the tears well up in her eyes. This was a young man, the same one who had approached me earlier in the day. I told the woman he had given me the name Mark in the afternoon and asked who that was. The man next to her put his hand up and I told him that his son told him to call him Mack. The man nodded that I was correct. I then asked who the S name might belong to, and the younger woman put her hand up. This was his sister, who told me her name was Sarah, the same name I had heard before the show. I could have kicked myself for not just saying it! The D name was for his mother Dianne. Then he traced a big C. That was his initial, his mum told me with a smile.

I knew it was a different name. I tried but failed. I think I said Carl. His mum told me his name was Chris but everyone called him Cookie. My head started to pound, which to me signifies head injuries usually brought about by a car accident. I was told he had sustained a head injury a week before he died. I was confused. I was sure my afternoon visitor had had a car accident. He told me that he was responsible and that alcohol was involved.

By now Dianne had more tears in her eyes as she said yes. This is where I thought that maybe I had been wrong in the afternoon and this young man had not passed in an accident but had in fact committed suicide. So I left it for a bit. Once again, he reminded me of the football. I relayed this and it too was correct.

Cookie displayed how tall and good-looking he was and showed me a picture of himself to prove that statement. I relayed the message to his mum who smiled and agreed. Then Cookie showed me another picture where I saw that he had dark hair and blue eyes. His mum was agreeing with everything I was saying.

Now the pounding was back. Cookie explained that he was in a vehicle accident and that it was his fault as he had been drinking and should not have been on the road. I relayed what he had told me to his parents and they nodded.

He told me his mum had his ring and again he told me the number 18. I asked his mother if that was his age and she said no. He was insisting that it was relevant. It turned out that he passed away two days after their wedding anniversary, which was on the 18th of the month. He explained that he had passed three years earlier. This was correct and as I looked at Dianne's face, I could see it was etched with the raw pain of grief. I had to control my emotions. It does me no good to go into the pain of any of my clients.

I had heard the name Terry a few times and told his parents. They told me he was a friend of theirs. Cookie told me he had someone with him that was close to Terry. Dianne told me that Terry had also lost a son. The son's name was Jason and he took over from Cookie to tell me that he had also crossed over in an accident and that although he and Cookie had not known each other in life, they were mates now. He also wanted them to pass on love to his dad who had still not come to grips with his son's death. There were more validations and lots of love sent out. I could see the family's weight lifted off their shoulders. They had found their son and he was in the company of a treasured family friend's son.

On other occasions it is the family who has been led to me. I regularly conduct short readings on radio. One night, a nurse was driving to work her midnight shift and tuned in. She was also a bereaved mother and had recently sought out a psychic in her local area, hoping for some validation from her son, Michael. During the reading, the psychic told her that the only message she could get was something like 'Whispers from Spirit' or 'Spirit Whispers.' The psychic had been uncertain about the message and the woman went home a little disappointed.

That night whilst driving to work, she had been feeling a little lower than usual and decided to turn on the radio to listen to some music. That is when she heard me on the air and listened. She was amazed at the messages being given one after the other that were validated every time. She later told me that when the radio announcer mentioned my website: www.spiritwhispers.org, she finally understood the message her son had been trying to relay to her. She felt that he had been trying to get her to make an appointment with me. When the appointment day finally came, it proved to be a most rewarding reading. Her son had chosen me and once again, I was humbled beyond belief that the spirit world had sought me out to undertake this exceptional spirit connection.

These are just a few examples of how the spirit world calls me, and they have always stood out in my mind. It has always struck me how often it is the spirit children that will seek me out in this manner, actually pressuring me for weeks and sometimes months, to lead me to their parents. I have often felt that it is because of my understanding and the loss of my own daughter, Crystal, that encourage them to do so. I feel very special knowing that they trust me in such delicate situations. The persistence these kids manifest to convince me to be in any one place cannot be ignored. It truly shows how strong the bond of love between parent and child is and proves to me time and time again that this sacred bond cannot ever be broken, even through the tragic circumstance of death.

I shall never forget Crystal's intervention from the spirit world to get me back on track, and it seems that most spirit children really do want their parents to know that they are around. Reading sessions involving children are usually emotional but healing. I feel it is wonderful that there is now an option for open-minded parents to seek out a qualified medium and be reunited. I am furthermore convinced that the spirit world is also happy with the emergence of gifted mediums to enable them to let their families know that they are okay. As I have said before, it is truly humbling to know the spirit world has trusted me with this amazing gift.

Chapter 10

During public demonstrations, mediums are directed where to go by the spirit world. I have tried to read for those who looked like they needed a reading, only to be very disappointed in the results. After the shows, I am often asked why a person's spirit didn't come through. One answer is that other spirits were a little more persistent, or else that the spirit world felt someone else needed the validation more in order to help them get back onto the right path.

No matter how big the crowd is, the spirit world will get to you when it feels it will help the most. A woman had been attending shows since her son had crossed over, but he waited almost two years to come through. I have a feeling that each show his mother had attended had prepared him to communicate clearly. It was interesting to note that his aunt was the one who opened the door for him to communicate. I wonder if he had been a little nervous and needed his aunt to guide him. When a young spirit stumbles during a reading, an older relative in spirit will often take over for a while until the young spirit calms down. Because they wish so much to let their family know they are fine, nervousness takes over. Not only are we learning about the validity of spirit communication, but the spirit world is also doing the same thing. If you have been disappointed that your spirit person did not come through, spare a thought for them and consider that they may in fact have been there all along, picking up tips on how to communicate with you at a later date.

So please walk to each show with an open heart and accept that your loved ones may also be there for the first time, picking up tips. Remember that the spirits that come through may be a little quicker at picking up communication skills, or may have been studying them for longer. If you do this, you will spare yourself a lot of disappointment, should your loved one not come through. Also keep the energy in the room on a high vibrational level by accepting each reading as validation that the spirit world is only a whisper away.

Another worry people have is that their spirits have been deceased for a long time and may not come through. It has been proven to me time and again that this fear is unfounded.

The next reading clearly shows that there is no 'expiry date' and that sometimes secrets can be revealed.

I recently did a reading for a woman who had questions relating to her great grandfather. She had specific questions concerning his death and I quickly asked her to let him tell me. As I tuned in, I found his life had ended abruptly many years before. He gave me the name Ron and told me he had six children. It was then that I saw a sign I had never seen before. I could see this spirit standing with a rifle in front of him. He was standing on the edge of the ocean, a cliff edge. I could see that it was night-time and that he had a defensive stance. I felt that he was defending himself.

I went in a bit deeper and found this man had been drinking and gambling the night of his death and I then saw his body. This man's life had been taken. He had died trying to defend himself. After the reading had been completed, I asked the woman how he had died. At the time, it had been ruled as accidental but in my vision it was not. Many years had passed since his death, but this man was still very keen for the truth to be known.

Parents are the only people in the world who know us back to front. They know the silly us, the crazy us, the sensible us, and still love us, not matter what we do. They have watched us grow up, have celebrated our triumphs and dried our eyes in dark times, and generally made us the people we are today. We all miss our mums and dads when they go home to spirit. We miss the comfort of having them around and being our support systems, but the truth is we live our life knowing that our mums and dads will most likely cross over before us. Although it hurts at the time, I feel the majority of us accept this type of passing more readily than that of our children. In the years I've been a medium, I have been drawn to the spirit children and I am usually very successful in bringing them through.

In a surreal kind of way, I get to know them on a very personal level and these last two readings go down in my 'memorable reading file.'

This particular spirit lived in outback Australia in one of the towns I visited twice in my regional tour. His mother was sitting in the audience holding her breath. She had met mediums before but none had correctly said his name, and this was the only validation she required. However, her son did come through that night with a whole lot more information than she bargained for.

I was at the wrong place initially and was asking for the name Alan. The lady I was addressing kept saying no. Then I received the name Paul and the name Alan again as well as a tattoo.

A man sitting two rows up put up his hand and said that he thought this reading was for him. His name was Paul, his middle name Alan and he had a tattoo in his son's honour. His son told me he had passed in an accident and that his father and himself had the same middle name. He then told me to acknowledge another 'A' name, which turned out to be Amanda, his girlfriend at the time. The accident had only occurred a few years earlier. He then told me that someone with an R name had recently had a celebration he had attended in his spirit form. It was an engagement party for his cousin.

He gave me the names of several of his family members including his sister, his aunt, his aunt's boyfriend, and his mum. Then he mentioned a ute and gave a B name. It turned out that his sister's boyfriend had just bought a new ute. When his father sat in it, he said to the boy how much his son would have loved the colour. He then mentioned a fishing boat and a cap and later told me how he had two memorials, which proved to be correct: a special park bench memorial had been put up in his honour.

He told me that a baby would be born any day and then he sent a special message to Paul's brother Noel,. who was a firm sceptic. Then I heard the name Michael. I said to his mum that her son's name was Michael but everyone called him Mick. As I told her those words, tears filled her eyes. She had finally received the only validation she wished for.

It is so hard to lose a child. I cannot say this enough. With every parent I meet, I honestly wish they could see through my eyes and hear through my ears. If they could, they would know for sure that their child is still here, just a whisper away, in the next dimension.

I remember when I was gaining acceptance of my daughter's death, in the days before I realised I was a medium, I would pretend that she was simply in another country. I pretended that the language she spoke was too hard for me to understand, and that the only reason I could not see her was because I had not yet been issued the passport to travel to this magical land.

Now that I am a medium, I know for sure that we can all learn the language of spirit, and we do not have to be psychic to do so. The spirit world communicates with us on a constant basis, right within our physical world. If we really try hard to understand that our kids are still here and make the decision to learn the language of spirit, then we will know for sure that we do not have to miss those who are definitely still around. This thought had been frustrating me since I first started readings.

The signs became very obvious to me and I knew that if I could help grieving parents and family members to identify them, they too could continue their relationships with their kids on a new level. So as time went by, the seed grew and with each reading where I brought a child through, it gained strength. One reading that particularly touched me involved a young man who had committed suicide.

Chapter 11

Suicide is perhaps one of the most tragic ways that someone can pass over to the spirit realms. The remaining family members are left to wade through their feelings of guilt, anger, disbelief and unanswered questions. Eventually, most accept that this was out of their hands and let time do the healing, but some find themselves frozen in grief years later, and that is where a medium can be of great value.

The worst case I witnessed was a woman who sat before me nervously screwing her handkerchief in her hands. I could see that grief was destroying her and the worried look on her daughter's face confirmed it. I already knew a young male who had committed suicide was present in the room. He had been with me since early that morning, anxious for me to help his poor mother. I knew he had been around for a couple of days, as I had not stopped seeing the number 919, which has become my 'suicide number.'

As I tuned in, I saw a young man walking down a busy street. He had plain looks and bad acne. His hands were in his jacket's pockets, and as people approached him, he seemed to shrink inwards and avert his eyes not to make eye contact. There was an air of depression around him, and my heart sank when he snuck a look at a pretty girl. He dared not let her see him looking; such was his fear of rejection. This young man had been rejected many times before and he could take no more. His demeanour showed that he had given up on life, happiness and love. This young man wanted out of this life and unfortunately he now was. His name was John and he committed suicide by hanging. He showed me himself being picked on and taunted by other boys and sadly, being alone for most of his school life. I had tears in my eyes as he relayed how lonely he truly had been. He craved acceptance and most of all, he craved the love of a woman, any woman, but unfortunately no one had ever looked twice at him.

In my heart, I could feel his sheer desperation and his fear of enduring this long life without ever really feeling the love he longed for. In his mind there was nothing but a desolate and empty future ahead. Perhaps if the kids at school had accepted him, his life would have taken a different path, but kids being kids had made his lonely life unbearable. He had struggled with himself for years. Despite being surrounded by a very loving family, he would while away the hours in the pain of never being accepted for himself by his peers. In a strange way, I totally understood why he had committed this act.

This was one thing I could never admit to his mother. She kept crying and asking me how her son, her much loved son, could possibly do this to her or to himself. I tried to explain that he just didn't like himself and she cried at me that she loved him. Why couldn't he see that? I explained to her that he knew that, but his strong dislike of himself had brought him to this point. I continued the reading and validated it was really him by things that he had done during his short life. Everything he told me was confirmed and although his mother understood his loneliness, she told me that she felt her love was enough for him and that it should have sustained him for his life. I sensed that John had somehow instigated the reading as he wanted her to know how much he loved her and that he was very much still around. When the reading ceased, exhaustion flooded every part of me and I truly realised that this young man had been beside himself looking for ways to help his mum. I was unsure how much the reading had helped, so I sent healing energy every night to that family.

One day, about three months later, my assistant received a call from this mother. She explained that the reading had helped her very much and that she had started to see signs of John around. The only question she had was if he knew that they were moving.

If so, would he be in her new house as well? Even though at first it felt like no good had come from the reading, it ended up being successful. I am positive that young John must have been very happy that his mum finally reached acceptance.

I've had many readings involving suicide in the past few years, many different events surrounding each one. Their decision has often been on the spur of the moment. Almost all of these cases have been young men in their late teens or early twenties. Two of them smashed their car and in fear of the consequences just killed themselves instead, to the total devastation of their families. Others, like young John, felt they didn't fit in this world.

No matter whether a child is lost to suicide or to any other cause, it's always a very hard time for the parents. After the reading and the initial euphoria of making contact were over, my clients quickly descended back into deep grief. They had too many questions left unanswered, and as much as I would like to answer them in a reading, there is rarely enough time.

Most of them were still stuck in the moment, unable to let go of the death. They were not accepting, nor did they understand why their loved ones were gone; a lot of them wasting years lost in grief. This grief was driven by the guilt they felt to have wasted precious time with their loved ones. They were now wasting present moments they could be enjoying with remaining family members and friends. Some were hell-bent on blaming others for the death. Their unforgiving nature was causing them to continually feel angry and look back with sadness.

This type of behaviour is far from what our spirit people want. If we can learn to let go of such behaviour and live in the moment, then it is a certainty that we will see the signs our spirit people send us every single day. When we continually live in anger and remorse, our vibrations operate at a very low level. If you consider that the spirit world vibrates on a much higher level, then it makes sense that if we wish to receive signs, we must let go of low vibrational behaviour such as anger, revenge, guilt and unforgiving practices.

I was a perfect example of guilt and grief destroying my life.

I used everything my guides taught me in the early days and some teachings from my favourite authors to design my first one-day seminar. I have found that this seminar can be very helpful for mothers and fathers trying to make sense of the loss of their child. In this school of Life, losing a child is the hardest of all lessons to survive and grow from. It is apparent that some will never move past the death and be frozen in grief for the remainder of their lives. Working as a medium has led me to some very sad parents and to some very loving spirit children who only wish for their parents to heal.

In August 2006, I toured with two other mediums. During the last of the trio of shows, a woman in the audience was waiting patiently as she had done for many shows prior to this one. Unlike the majority of audience members, she knew the chances that she would receive a reading were slim. She remained hopeful, but as the night carried on, her heart sank lower.

This was a woman tormented by suicidal thoughts day in and day out. Her son, Steven, had been tragically killed in an accident two years earlier, and her life had been a nightmare ever since. He was hit by a car and killed instantly on his way home from school. This young boy had been the light of his parents' world. With a passion for sport, he had been a rising star in his soccer team. There were other children in the family, but his poor mother was finding it a huge struggle to stay on Earth without her son, Steven.

It was the last reading of the night and I was drawn to a table at the back. I said I had a Donna with me in the spirit realms. I pointed to a woman with a white blouse and said I thought I was with her, but still she had no idea until her husband reminded her that he had a sister in spirit named Donna. When I told him she died due to meningitis as a child, he looked stunned and agreed. I gave him more validations then asked who the big C name was. He shook his head, but then his wife asked if it could be an S, as she was looking for her son Steven. I immediately felt a young boy near me who had crossed over due to a head trauma and this was confirmed. Steven mentioned a portrait of him and how he had been good at soccer, that his mum always wore a chain around her neck with his picture on it, and many more details. Most importantly, he was okay.

This was not enough for Steven's mum. In subsequent phone calls, she revealed she was concerned that Steven may be crying for her. She spent many days in bed with tissues, drowning in her own tears. Despite my frequent phone calls, her grief had become destructive.

Chapter 12

The death of a loved one is a catalyst for change. It is the soul's chance to experience grief and grow in its eternal advancement. When someone dies it is natural to grieve. However, as with all other life experiences, we have a choice. Will our grief be constructive or destructive?

There are certain stages of grief we all travel through depending on the nature of the death. For an accident or sudden death, you can expect shock, denial, anger and guilt. These emotions will be experienced in a fog-like state, and can cause memory loss and depression for a period of time after the death. Accepting this type of death is a tough process because there is no chance to say goodbye.

In the case of terminal illness, the same emotions will be felt before the death. However, there will be a chance to redeem guilt and say goodbye. By the time the loved one has passed away, sadness and of course a longing for their physical presence remains. Acceptance is somewhat easier as it is terrible to see someone we love in pain. To know they are free of pain can be comforting.

When grief is affecting the way we respond to remaining family members and friends, then it is time to seek help. It is normal to think of our loved ones in spirit for the rest of our lives and to experience depression around birthdays and anniversaries. However, after a certain amount of time, this depression should decrease.

I remember the ninth anniversary of my daughter's death passing peacefully, but in the tenth year, I became so depressed that I pleaded for the day off work. It was because of the milestone factor of a decade passing. Grief can hit you at the strangest times and for many years later, but if it remains quite random then this would be considered normal.

Parents who have lost a child can be caught up in the emotional rollercoaster of grief for much longer than others, especially when there was no chance to say goodbye. Quite often, parents will look outside of themselves to find relief and indulge in substance abuse. This can be very destructive as it can lead to further problems with remaining family members. Unhealed grief can cause a breakdown in the family unit, leaving the remaining children to question their own existence, especially if one parent rejects them in favour of staying in the moment of death.

Too often, people begin to identify themselves with the pain and continually remind anyone who will listen how unfortunate they are because they lost a child. Eventually, they feel such self-sympathy that they cease to exist anywhere but in the moment of death, trapped deep within a painful memory. They stop working. They cease to groom themselves and refuse to socialise. They might feel guilty to smile or laugh, so in order to stay true to the memory of their child, they refuse to do anything that resembles fun. While this behaviour is acceptable for the first six to twelve months, if it persists consistently any longer then it is self-destructive.

Some find themselves surrounded by memories of their loved ones constantly. The family home and local shops become a memory lane and each step taken through it is engrossed in the deep pain of how life used to be.

In severe cases of memory related grief, it may be advisable to move to a different area. I know a woman who moved and built a new home but insisted on including a room tailor-made for her deceased daughter. Her daughter had been gone for eight years. This type of grief is the most destructive of all. It is very important that you seek counselling should you feel this way. It is wise to remember that you will not connect to every counsellor you talk to. If you are a grieving mother, you may find it easier to identify with a male simply because you may resent the fact that another woman cannot possibly understand how you feel if she has not lost a child. A male counsellor will give you similar advice but you may feel more comfortable because he never was and never will be a mother. The most important thing is not to give up trying to find the right one.

When my daughter died, I found myself obsessed about whether I had been a good enough mother. The truth is that I was very young and self-absorbed when she was alive. I would toss and turn every night with this fear of not having been good enough. The guilt was destroying me. I eventually allowed my grief to become constructive and six months after her death, I enrolled in a community childcare course to see for myself how I rated as mother. I received the highest recorded marks and went on to volunteer in a childcare centre for a short time. Taking this action proved to me that I had little to be guilty about and helped immensely in my recovery.

I found that exercising helped to alleviate the anger I was storing. Grief can become physical and cause blockages in the energy system of the body. Exercise unblocks the system and releases endorphins in the brain to promote a feeling of wellbeing and happiness. A good diet ensures that the body gets the correct nutrients to counteract the negative effect of grief. This is very important in the case of a tragic and unexpected death. Try to watch how much you drink and smoke, as it is easy to lose track of the quantities you are consuming. This will invariably lead to more problems physically and emotionally later on.

I know of other mothers who have become involved in charities to ease their grief. A mother whose son passed with Leukaemia actively raises money for the Leukaemia Foundation. There are many ways that you can help yourself by helping others. The choice is yours.

Recovering from the death of a lifelong partner can be just as devastating.

Mary had been married to Wonga for 45 years before his health deteriorated to the point of death. She had faithfully nursed him for the past three years and when he passed away was plunged into a deep depression. Not only did she have too much time on her hands, but she was also missing his presence to the point where her family was very concerned. Mary was not recovering. Two years after his death, she was still crying every day and found it hard to get out of bed. She could see no reason for living without her beloved Wonga. The kids had grown up and had their own lives, and she didn't want to bother anyone.

Wonga had other ideas though.

One day, I found the whole family before me for a reading. He had been a strong male who always put others before himself and his whole family had learned from his example. Even when he was sick, he would rouse at the nurses to go and look after the kids and leave him to it. Every message he sent was confirmed with tears or laughter. He knew that Mary missed him greatly but he wanted her to pull herself together. He told me proudly that Mary and her daughter Debbie had recently started volunteering their time in a nursing home. This, he claimed, was the best medicine for Mary. And it was.

After the reading, Mary stopped crying everyday and, encouraged by her husband from the spirit realms, put even more effort into her time at the nursing home. I have kept in close contact with the family since, and these days Debbie helps me out. Mary is often found at the door at my shows handing out flyers and tickets. You would never know she was the same woman I met almost two years ago. Thanks to her family, her grief became constructive. They encouraged her to put her time to use and stopped her wallowing in her grief.

No matter how close your family is, every member will experience the death of a loved one in a different manner. Some will accept the death a lot more easily than others. Some will be thrown into depression. There are many factors involved, but what is important to remember is not to judge anyone's reaction by comparing it to your own. If someone seems to be coping better than you do, it does not mean they do not feel the pain of the loss or that you had deeper feelings. It is important at this time to try to keep the family unit as close as possible. If you want to see a medium but your family doesn't, don't force the issue. Let them grieve in their own way.

However, if you feel that a family member is not recovering, do not pull away. Remind them you are there for them, and if necessary seek professional help. Try to take extra time with them to help alleviate their pain. Take them out and think of ways to make their grief constructive. It is amazing what can be achieved if the family works as a team. Too often I have sat before clients that have felt abandoned by their family. This was one of Steven's mum's problems. Her sisters had got on with their lives and did not wish to hear about Steven anymore. Her mother had already passed away, so part of her inability to heal was a sense of abandonment.

Remember that we all have a choice with how we grieve. Some may never heal and that might be their life path. If you do want to recover, try to stay in the present and not wade back to 'what if' and 'if only' thoughts. This will help immensely. When you are in a melancholic mood thinking about your loved one in spirit, ask yourself if your grief is constructive or if you are being destructive?

The reason people grieve too much is simply because of a lack of understanding. Too many questions and not enough answers. We seek answers in the physical world and often come away with unfulfilling replies. While we live daily in a physical world with physical goals, we also live in a spiritual world. Our souls are also on a journey. It's only when we view life from the perspective of the next dimension that this physical life we are living becomes easier to understand.

Chapter 13

Even though you live a physical life on Earth, your soul is always connected to the Source. Without realising it, we constantly communicate with souls in our soul groups and secondary soul groups. This is apparent in a situation when we think of someone we haven't seen for a while and then bump into him or her on the street. Or the phone rings and we know who it is. This is the time that our souls are communicating.

Dreaming is a way that the spirit world can communicate with you. When spirits appear in dreams, it is a visit from the realms and it is very important to try to remember everything they say to you. Sometimes it may not be pleasant information. When I have heard people's fears about the words that were spoken, I have found the client was interpreting incorrectly. Spirits usually do not speak and when they do, it will only be a few lines.

I dreamed of my father after his death and he said four sentences. The first one was: "Do you know where you are going?" - "Stop right here." - "Don't go any further." These sentences were referring to my drug problem. At the time, I was out of control and I feel this was Dad's way of trying to warn me. This dream was four months before my boys were taken away from me, and eight months before I started to hear voices. The last sentence was: "Yes, I am home now." In the dream, Dad's face was radiant and as he said those words, I found deep peace. It strengthened my belief that there is nothing to fear about death.

Not everyone has dreams of those in spirit and the dreams do not occur often, but they are real visits. If you consider that we are spirits having a human experience, then it makes sense that when we dream, our spirits are freed from the physical restraints of life.

What better time for those we love to visit?

If you are not dreaming of a loved one and someone else is, you need to ask yourself if perhaps you are holding onto your grief a little too tight. Heavy grieving can impede spirit communication. Try to keep in mind the fact that your people are safe and still around. In fact, they are closer than you may know. Talk to them and tell them you wouldn't mind a dream visit. Remember if you are caught up in the moment of death to be aware that the dream may reflect your feelings rather than the spirit's feelings.

I have found that people who think too much about the way their loved ones died, and base their grieving process around the moment of death, find it hard to receive messages from them. It is important to take time to reminisce the good times rather than stay in the moment when it all ended. By focussing on that one moment, you are denying many more special moments with others, and also missing signs that your 'living' spirit is sending you.

Spirits vibrate on a high level and must lower their vibrations to communicate with a medium. Mediums must raise their vibrations. When mediums are tuned in, they consciously empty their mind of all personal thoughts. This allows spirits to telepathically transmit their own thoughts and feelings to the medium. If the medium is bogged down with personal thoughts, the connection will be distorted and the reading will not fare well.

There are many steps that you can take to ensure you remain open to messages being sent to you by raising your vibrations. Most importantly you should strive to remain positive and refrain from low vibrational behaviour such as anger, guilt and unrelenting grief. Keep in mind you will be meeting with your loved ones again and future lives are a definite possibility.

To raise your vibrations, you need to address any issues you may be holding onto. If you need to forgive yourself or others, do so. It doesn't mean you have to let those who hurt you back into your life, but forgiving them will help you. Always remember that you can hate someone as much as you like, but hate is a negative emotion that will eat you up and break you down. The person you hate may not even be aware of your feelings, so the only person who suffers is you.

It is wise to try to stay in the present moment. If you keep thinking about the past or worrying about the future, your present moment will be filled with anxiety and tension, thereby casting you into lower vibrations. When I find myself doing this, I simply direct my thoughts to my breathing. I focus on the breath filling my lungs and then exhaling from my body. You only need to do this for a few moments to help erase anxious thoughts from you mind.

Meditation will help you to relax and stay in the present. There are many different ways you can meditate and there are countless guided meditations you can purchase. There are also moving meditations such as Yoga, Chi Gung and Tai Chi. I would recommend that you start with guided meditation and then progress. My favourite is the breathing meditation practised by the Buddhists. I went to a silent meditation retreat called 'Vipassana' to learn it. This form of meditation teaches you to live in the moment by observing your breath and then by observing sensations in the body without reacting to them. I went for a ten-day retreat. I must say this was the hardest task I have ever taken on voluntarily, but one of the most effective, in teaching me to accept any situation without being hard on myself if something doesn't work out.

Diet and exercise can play an important part in spirit communication. Late last year, I was approached by a woman who felt that her son was attracting spirits. He was quite alarmed by it all. It can be very daunting when you are woken up by the spirit world, and often our first reaction will be fear. I spoke to this young man and found his mother's statements to be true. I gave him a few hints to get a good night sleep. As they did with me, the spirit world chose to communicate with this young man in the wee hours of the morning. He was working during the day and was simply not coping. I suggested to him to have something sweet, as it would disable the communication.

I discovered this when I started my Australian tour. After each show, I would have spirits visiting me till the wee hours. One night after a show, I had a slice of mud cake and was surprisingly given some peace. I tried it again and it worked! When I asked my guides, they told me that sugar lowers your vibrations, and mediums need to raise their vibrations to communicate. So knowing that sugar can actually help you to tune out has been a useful tool for me, and also a perfect excuse to eat mud cake. On the other hand, if you wish to remain open to spirit communication, it would be wise to stay away from high fat and high sugar foods as they will make you sluggish.

The spirit world always lives in the present moment. If you consciously make an effort to stay positive and live in the present, then you are doing exactly as your loved ones in spirit are doing. While living in the present moment, you will start to notice signs from spirit everywhere. You may notice that certain numbers keep popping up. They may be relevant to a birth date or anniversary, but do not be mistaken in thinking this is coincidental. If you suspect it is, ask a friend how often they see the same sequence. It may surprise you that the birth and anniversary numbers of your loved ones are only around for you. I suggest that you ask your spirits to make this a form of communication. You may notice certain animals around when you think of your spirit people. Pay attention to see if it happens often. At times, you may be driving and when you look up, see a street sign with the name of someone you care for. If they are in spirit, it will mean they are close. If they are still alive, I would suggest you call them. It may mean that they need love at this particular time.

This is the way I communicate with my own family in spirit. When I think I hear my family in spirit, I tend to think it is wishful thinking on my behalf and that I am hearing what I want to hear. When I communicate with a client's spirit, the client is validating what I am hearing, but when I have my own spirits on board, I only have myself to validate the information. For the very same reason, I cannot read for friends or family members because I may be relaying information already known to me. This is why I use numbers and animals to reassure myself that my family members are with me when I need them. Once you start to work with spirit, you will find many unique forms of communication.

Mediums receive many messages through visions and this is also how we communicate with people of different nationalities. For instance, when a spirit shows me a car, I know it is a car and although it may be called different things in different languages, it will always look like a car. So in the case of different languages, the spirit usually knows to resort to my clairvoyance abilities. It is important to recognise that most mediums do not actually see spirits; it is more like seeing a memory. If you practice meditation, you may find your clairvoyant abilities will strengthen. You may even see your spirit people whilst relaxing in a meditative state. If you are consciously trying to stay in the present, then trust that what you are seeing is in real time. Do not dismiss it as a memory.

The sense of touch is one favoured by spirit. It is called clairsentience. When I conduct a show, clairsentience is one of my major senses. In a two hour period, I will feel as if I am having a heart attack, getting run over, suffering from cancer, strangling, drowning and so on. I actually feel these sensations physically. They do not hurt me or cause permanent damage. They are a mild indicator of what the spirits suffered before they passed.

If someone was feeling this but did not understand, I can only imagine they would be very scared. As people are 'waking up,' they are developing this sense and I am urging you to think sensibly about what is happening. Do not assume you have an evil spirit there. It may be your grandma just letting you know she is around. She may be delighted that you can actually feel her and is possibly testing to see how far you can develop. So if you start to feel the spirit world around or perhaps see or hear them, please do not run off in search of an exorcist, keep calm, meditate and perhaps ring a reputable medium to see if this is in fact your gift developing. Take the word evil and negative out when thinking of the spirit world. Live strong in your light and do not let this world take the beauty out of our loving spirit.

Chapter 14

When we die, we drop our physical shells and our souls return to the realms. We will be met by our guide or our loved ones and then be reunited with our soul group. There is much joy when a spirit returns home and they will be surrounded in a festive atmosphere by the souls of the people they love. I imagine this reunion would be one of elation and relief.

My clients often express concern about whether they will recognise everyone, and a question I am often asked is whether children age in the spirit world. As a mother who has lost a child, I know that I would much prefer to be greeted by my daughter's four year old incarnation when I cross over.

I remember early in my career, I was reading for a lady who had lost her son from cot death and I told her I could see a three-year-old boy in my vision. He was very precise with his validations and everything was met with a yes. When I said the boy was three, I thought he died at the age of three. She explained to me that he would have been three at the time of the reading, but he had passed away at nine months old.

Another woman I read for had been the driver of the car that killed her seven-year-old daughter. When the daughter came through, she presented herself as twenty-eight, the age she would have been then. In other readings, I will be given both ages.

Any parent who has lost a child can usually tell you immediately how old their deceased child would be. It is my understanding that the spirit world demonstrates the current age to bring comfort and validation to the parent during the reading.

I have realised that the soul is ageless, and that no matter how old we are, we still feel the same inside. Ultimately it is the soul essence I am able to communicate with, the part of the spirit that makes us all individuals. I truly believe that each individual soul is evolving and growing at different rates and continues to do so after physical death. There is one definable thing that makes us unique, and I am of the opinion that it stays with us for each incarnation we take on, whether we incarnate as male or female.

So back to the question, yes, it seems that they do age but perhaps not in the way that we would understand on Earth. I feel that when we die, we will be welcomed by the people we said goodbye to, no matter how many years have passed.

When we arrive home to spirit, our soul memories, which were de-activated at the time of birth, will be reactivated. We will then have full recall of every life we have lived. Most importantly, we will completely understand the contract of the life just left behind. There will be a life review and it will be compared to all of our past lives to establish whether we attained our goals. This is a very important part of the soul's journey.

The spirit world will not judge us should we fail in our previous life. Our guides will be on hand to offer us possible alternatives we could have taken and will also point out our strengths. If there was judgement, souls would be unwilling to reincarnate and life as we know it would cease. It is the intent of every soul to be perfect, and to attain perfection, so compassion and understanding of every life situation is necessary, good and bad. Our guides and teachers in the spirit realm have experienced what we have and help us assess the best course of action in future lives. They do this without judgement or prejudice and steer us with love and compassion as they have done since the time our individual soul was created.

Time does not exist in the spirit realms. The only time is now. Right now! While we are in spirit we have full access to Earth and are able to observe our remaining family members at leisure. We continue to learn how our life impacted our family from the spirit world. Spirits also try to communicate with their remaining family members to help alleviate their grief. Many mediums have been awoken in order to give messages to the living, as far too many people aren't aware of the communication happening. In readings, they tell me how they have travelled with their Earth families and will give intricate details of events that have happened since they passed over.

Some spirits have told me how they have visited places on Earth after their death. There were two young spirits who told me that they had travelled together to Paris to observe life in nightclubs. I feel spirits spend time studying earthly occupations as well. For instance, a soul with healing energy might study Earth doctors to establish where they might like to direct future incarnations. A musical soul may study musicians to get a feeling of where music may be heading. Everything we know on Earth is known in the spirit realm.

While in the spirit world, we choose our future life and we utilise members of our soul groups and secondary soul groups to play important roles. It is a highly organised procedure and much care is taken to ensure all of the souls involved are catered for. Some may have to return in their next incarnation to balance out bad karma. I suspect these would be the people that are deemed misfits in our current society or those that didn't choose wisely in their previous lives. The point is that future lives are a chance to redeem our souls and learn the lessons from previous bad behaviour on Earth.

When we choose a future life, we also choose the way we would like to look and a personality that will best suit us to learn our chosen lessons. Basically, we are a soul first and a human ego second. We choose our human form in much the same way as an actor would choose a character to play. For instance, an actor can play a villain or a hero and each part will differ greatly. However, because it is the same actor, the essence of the actor can be found in every part they play. Similarly, our soul essence will be present in every life we live even though our incarnations will greatly differ.

Our Earth family members may be made up of souls who are working at different levels. I have felt for a long while that my daughter is a more advanced soul than I am. In life, she was very loving and non-judgemental. She was also my greatest teacher. Our soul mates can be our lovers, brothers or sisters, best friends and even our parents. In one life we may choose to be siblings and the next life we may choose to be partners. The important thing to remember is to not limit oneself by dismissing the possibilities.

Sometimes we meet someone for the first time and we feel we have known him or her forever. This is a sure sign that you have met a member of your soul group and usually these individuals will play an important role in your life for a period of time. They will teach us lessons through love or fear. Whichever way it is, the people who impact you most and teach you the most in whatever manner, usually have a soul contract with you.

Many of my clients worry that their loved ones in spirit may reincarnate before they reach them again. In most cases, I feel that this fear is unfounded. If you feel a very close bond with a deceased family member, the chances are you have a strong soul connection. If this is so, then it is apparent you will spend many lives together. There seems to be no set time between incarnations and spirits do not have to reincarnate until they feel ready. In most cases, there is quite a long time between lives, even in the case of suicide. I feel it may span over several Earth lifetimes because time has no relevance in the spirit realm. What seems like a lifetime to us may only be a weekend in the spirit world.

Chapter 15

The last quarter of 2006 was when my life began to tumble down. I had already toured fifty plus towns and was in more debt than I had ever been in my life. The tour with the other two mediums had helped a little, however, every day I woke up with a sick feeling in my stomach, wondering if I was ever going to break free from debt. Most spiritualists claim that if you look after spirit, spirit will look after you. Well, that didn't seem to be working with me!

I was unhappy at home. I was still living with my ex-boyfriend, Rebmen, and my oldest son, Alan. Alan had been coming on my tours for the past few months in an effort to cut costs, but he was not happy doing so and it affected my work on the road. Rebmen was a messy housemate and we often fought about the state of the house. Each time I set off on the road, I would tidy up and come back to an enormous mess. I wanted to move but the lack of money and a full credit card prevented me from taking that step. I was depressed and wondering about my sanity at undertaking such an enormous task.

Still I pressed on, and despite my flagging spirits set off to visit the same towns I had visited earlier in the year. I think I was quite insane. I was in the first leg of my second time round, when I got the news that mum had been taken to hospital and was in a very bad shape. I could not fight the fear in my heart anymore. It had been sleeping there gnawing at my insides for the past twelve months and had increased in the past three. My guides had been telling me that mum's time was almost over. I was totally distraught and wanted to cancel the rest of the tour. Mum told me to keep going. I remember sitting in the green room before the show on the night I heard about mum, when I felt a familiar presence. It was the same town where I had met the sceptic's son earlier in the year. The spirit was Paul and he told me he had offered my guides and family to help me with the show as apparently my spirit daughter and brother were needed by mum's side.

Five minutes to show time, and I was a mess. I had tears running down my face with grief and tears of thankfulness for Paul's kind offer. The show went well despite my pain and Paul proved to be a most wonderful guide on the night.

Mum came home from hospital and I relaxed a little. I told myself my previous fears were just paranoia. The spirit world knew how much I needed my mum; they would not let her die yet. Mum and I were a team. She even answered the phones when Mandy was away. For the first time in a long while mum was enjoying her new role as my part time assistant. She was easily able to answer phones from her bedside where it seemed that she needed to spend a lot of time. She made friends and with her vast knowledge of grief she was able to counsel and reassure the many distraught people who called daily.

It was still a busy time and I conducted my Healing workshop and had the pleasure of both Sharon and Deanne in the same room. Lynette, Daniel's sister, also attended and the day was successful in terms of making people see death in a new light.

In October, I continued on the same trek. It seemed I had toured too closely between shows and in each town, the numbers were getting smaller and smaller. My son hated it and grew more sullen with each passing kilometre. We drove on and on through one drought affected town after another, each one producing more tales of hardship and despair. The number of readings where suicide was involved increased dramatically at each show. It seemed everyone was doing it the hard way in 2006. I was digging deeper in debt but rising in understanding and compassion. With each town, there was always someone who made me count my lucky stars, and with each show my mum was quietly slipping away. I was trying to avoid her ever declining health and every day we spent hours on the phone thinking of ways we could make this tour work with no dollars.

With time, Alan decided he didn't want to travel anymore. I enlisted the help of Debbie, Wonga's daughter, and I still think this was one of my best decisions to date.

November proved to be the worst financial disaster of the lot. As bad as it was, I now had Debbie to cheer me up and she taught me how to laugh at it all. She was just the tonic I needed. We got off the plane for the last tour and although it was mid-November in Australia, we were freezing. We found a second-hand shop and bought winter woollies. Town after town, Deb's presence put a bright glow on this last leg for 2006. In a small town, we found ourselves in the smallest of motel rooms, bored out of our minds with no television. It was then that we started to recount 'the life and times of an Australian medium.' The excitement and thrill of it all – not! It seemed people thought we lived the high life, but eating frozen dinners cooked in motel rooms' microwaves while staring at the ceiling fantasising about how the 'successful' mediums could live, was not as high as they might think. But it was fun. We met some lovely, funny people along the way and at times, I even had to hold back what spirits were saying because of the town being so small.

In one town, there was a particularly huge man I was reading in the audience. He was 6 foot 5 inches high, definitely a biker and his face indicated he had partied the hard way. His friend in spirit was a very cocky man who had been murdered by a rival drug producing gang. He was very open with his validations. However, I was not so keen to tell the whole town about his activities, especially due to the possibility of his mate becoming a little upset. This man was way too big to tangle with. So I edited the reading but got everything right, his name and their association, as well as his description. I told the biker I would speak to him later and after the show, I told him the rest of the validations. Although the information was very damning, the big biker had tears in his eyes as he gave me a hug and thanked me for letting his mate come through. It seemed like his mate always had a bit of a big mouth and that is possibly why he found himself in this small town talking to me that night from the spirit side.

Then there was the small seaside town where we only had fifteen people in the audience. The strangest thing was that most of the patrons were looking for husbands who had either suicided or died in accidents. I have wondered if perhaps they needed to meet and my being there was a catalyst to do so. Deb and I often laugh out loud about those early days. It was a struggle but makes the now seem well deserved.

My mum was still to meet Deb and the opportunity came at a John Edward seminar. Mum had long wanted to see our hero and I had purchased tickets for her, Debbie, her mum and myself. Poor mum, it was such a struggle for her. She had been getting sicker and sicker but miraculously got better for the day. The security guards, however, were not happy to have her there. It seems that if you are sick and in a walker, you are considered a public liability risk. I have to give it to mum for getting us surrounded by big, good looking, 'beefy'men though. They never took their eyes off her. With Deb and her mum's help, we got mum settled into her seat and watched our idol on stage. He was not working at his best that night and mum, always my most devoted fan, told me that I had nothing to worry about: I was much better than John. I am not so sure about that. However, my mum loved me and in that moment I knew this was to be our last outing together.

After that night, mum's health continued to decline.

Chapter 16

A few weeks later, a little voice started singing. It wasn't a real song; it was more like a tune that was happy and content. The words were: 'Grandma, Grandma, Grandma!' and my spirit daughter, Crystal, was the singer. It started soft and got louder as the day went on. The panic in me started to rise, but I still stubbornly refused to acknowledge the truth. However, by the end of the day I no longer had a choice. By seven pm that night, I was by my mother's side. I had been told that I had two days left by the doctors *and* the spirit world.

In all the deaths that have occurred in my life, I had only received the opportunity to say goodbye once, and that was with my Grandfather. But even then, I was so torn up with the grief of my daughter's death that I did not take advantage of the situation and did not get to say it. Now I was sitting by my mother's bedside watching her struggle for breath, barely speaking. My stubborn mum insisted on staying home, and she also insisted on morphine. I knew what she was doing but I also knew she had had enough of struggling to breathe and not being able to walk on her own. I sat by my mum's side getting in the way. At intervals, I would take off and ring my friend Debbie to get her to talk me through it all. I was not coping. The last forty-eight hours seemed like a month.

I have never felt so totally useless and angry with myself. I wanted to make mum feel better, but we were past that stage and I knew it. The next night my mum lapsed into unconsciousness, but before she did she gave me a gift I have never let go. As a family we have never been the type to say 'I love you' or give each other cuddles. We are more the type that just knows the love is there. That night as I was watching my mum struggle for breath, I told her how much I loved her, and the very last words she spoke were: 'I love you too.' Some might take these words for granted, but to me they are more precious than the biggest diamond.

The next morning, I went to the shop to get a coffee and at the top of mum's road, I had a vision that filled the road. It was my brother Martin. He had his arms crossed and a stern look on his face. I knew he was here for mum, and I asked him how long it would be. He told me two. I thought he meant two hours, but it was not two hours, it was two pm.

At one- thirty, I felt this desperate need for a diet coke. It was like I would die of thirst if I didn't get it. I had been sitting with mum all day and from time to time, thoughts kept crossing my mind that perhaps my energy was holding onto her too tight.

When this craving started, I went to the toilet and asked Peter, my guide, if I should go get the drink. He asked me if I were prepared that my mum would cross over if I left. I asked him if it would help. When he told me it would, I left. I drove to the shop, bought the Coke and as I got back in the car, I called mum's house. I looked at my docket, and yes, she died the minute I purchased the Coke one fifty-seven pm, December 10, 2006.

Mum was only 63 years old, but she was finally free from the pain her lungs had inflicted on her all her life. She had never smoked, but like her father she had been born with malfunctioning lungs and that was ultimately her demise.

On that day, I didn't just lose my mother, I also lost my best friend and living guide. As you might imagine, I was devastated. Ten minutes after she died, she came to me. I had this most exhilarating feeling shoot through my whole being. It felt exciting, energetic, delirious and free all at once. Then she began to give me signs that Martin and Crystal were with her. This feeling only lasted a few minutes but it was one I will never forget. I have thanked her for sharing her walk through the gate with me. I began to cry and she immediately thumped me in the heart. It was clear that she was happy where she was.

The moment mum died, the child in me went with her. It was up to me now. I felt very alone. Who was going to get me through mum's death? Mum had held my hand through all the deaths I had encountered before and now she was gone. The complete and utter loneliness I felt was overwhelming. This woman was the first I had loved, the first I had seen when I opened my eyes as a baby, and now my human eyes could no longer see her.

I knew I would miss our long phone calls. Her complete acceptance and understanding of my complex nature was also gone. Yes, I knew she was there in spirit; she let me know that with touch, but I wanted to hear her voice, talk about her death with her. As adept as I am at communicating with other people's spirits, that is a luxury reserved purely for my clients and audience members.

The rest of the world believes I have one up in communication. I do not. I have a better understanding and I know she is around me. I see signs on a daily basis and she is constantly in my dreams. But the rest, I often perceive as wishful thinking and feel that I may be imagining it because the information is not coming from a third source.

I truly struggled after mum died. My business funds were at an all time low. I was now surviving purely on my credit card. I had to let go of my assistant, Mandy, as I could not afford to pay her any longer. I was in too much personal pain to do readings. It was also school holidays, so it was a hard time emotionally and financially.

Mum's service day fell six days after her death, the same day I was due to do a charity show. I told them the circumstances but they still tried to make me do the show. I explained that my mum's service was the same day and they asked if I could arrange another medium. It really hurt me, this was to be the third show for this group and I had donated all the proceeds from each show to them. I told them I just couldn't and that if they wanted to wait until January, I could do it then. The woman virtually hung up in my ear and told me not to worry about it, they would get another medium.

After all the grief I had dealt with in their groups free of charge, they just cut me off when I needed them. I haven't done a charity show since then. Hopefully in the future, I will be in a position to do so again.

January melted into February, and still I was finding it hard to cope. I was due to do another round of shows with the mediums I had worked with in 2006, so I threw myself into organising the Queensland events. I felt I should not cry because mum had been so ill and at least I got to say goodbye. I struggled on, digging deeper into debt and heading for another emotional breakdown.

It was around this time that I met one of my most memorable spirits. He and I would be best mates before long, and despite my grief, he needed me now.

Chapter 17

The hot summer wind blew through the back door and the Christmas tree toppled over. The decorations rolled away, scattering brightly over the floor. There were two specially printed Christmas ball decorations given by a mother to her two children. Out of all the decorations, only one had shattered. It was her son Tyson's. As she put the pieces in the bin, she had no idea the ball would not be necessary the following year.

The Turner family, a tight knit crew of four, had moved to Queensland in 1997 a year after Tania's dad, Barry, was tragically killed in an accident at the age of 55. His truck had come unstuck around a corner and had tipped over. A man following him had rushed to the scene, but had not been able to free Barry's legs and had to run for his own life to escape the explosion which claimed Barry's life. There was neither rhyme nor reason for the accident, and in the following ten years of searching, Tania never found a reasonable explanation.

As horrific as the event had been, there had been a small blessing in the fact that Tyson had not been in the truck with his grandfather that day as previously arranged. The accident had occurred on a school holiday. Instead of going on the promised trip with his grandfather, Tyson had opted to mow the lawn for pocket money. They were like two peas in pod and Tyson was shattered when he lost his old mate.

They decided that a change would pick the family up, and when they moved, Tyson began a love affair with motocross bike riding. He took to it like a duck to water and pursued his career with an enthusiasm and passion that would see him reach National levels.

Riding with broken bones to score points was part of his nature, as was stopping his bike to help a mate that had fallen off.

Tyson was popular with all his mates and also with the ladies. At age 19, he found himself in a hospital ward with his first-born son, Kaleb. It was a stressful time for the whole family, as Kaleb was born prematurely at twenty-three weeks. At six weeks old, he was diagnosed with moderate Cerebral Palsy.

As young as he was, Tyson supported his son one hundred percent. Eventually he and his partner moved in together to make a family life for his young son. Life was a struggle and Tania kept a close eye on the situation, lending a few dollars or buying some groceries when the young couple found it hard to cope.

Tyson tried hard to make it work but had it tough, as his partner's family were against the union from day one. Eventually, the fighting started. Drugs somehow got in the way, and Tyson eventually accepted he would never have the family life he envisioned. In March 2006, after many arguments and fights, the young couple was in court fighting for young Kaleb.

While Tyson was proving to be a responsible parent, spending time with Kaleb at the hospital for his physio, his partner was neglecting her parental duties. Tyson was awarded four days a week custody and moved in with his family. By this time, Tyson had become a regular pot smoker and occasional party drug user. It was little wonder really, considering the stress he had already endured in his young life. His family stuck by him and as a team, they ensured that young Kaleb received the best possible care.

In September 2006, Tyson celebrated his twenty-first birthday and Tania breathed a sigh of relief, thanking her lucky stars. All Tyson's life, she had this feeling that if she just got him to twenty-one then he would be okay.

Nonetheless, Tania still worried about her reckless son, and broached the subject one afternoon when she picked him up from work. She told him she was worried about his partying and suggested he slow down a little. He brushed her off in his good-natured way, said that she worried too much, and that he just wanted to have fun. Still Tania pushed at him. Her concern for his welfare had come alive and she told him to be careful, as she couldn't bear to lose him. "What about Kaleb?" she asked. If the worst happened, what did he want done? He laughed, and said to cremate him and get someone to do a special motocross jump and spread his ashes over the track.

These were fateful words. Destiny was speaking loud and clear and Tania didn't have a clue.

A little over two weeks later, Tyson embarked on another party weekend and Tania looked after young Kaleb. On the Saturday, he nearly drowned when his shoulder dislocated while water-skiing. On the Sunday, Tyson went out to a mate's place and then came back to collect his younger sister's car. It was unregistered and Tania suggested he hire a car trailer to move it to his mate's place.

Against his family's better judgement, he took the car and drove off with his mate, Steve, following in his own car. He grinned cheekily at his mum before he left and declared his love for her. She replied that she loved him too, and watched as he drove away.

The phone rang. It was her husband's workmate telling him he would be late to pick him up. One of his Christmas lights had blown out and he wanted to fix it first.

A few minutes later, the phone rang again. It was Steve's girlfriend. There had been a terrible accident.

Tyson was still, his breathing had stopped, an unlit cigarette in his hand. Tania screamed at the girl to apply CPR. The girl was beside herself; she was worried about injuring him further. Tania insisted she pull him out, it didn't matter about further injuries. A police officer took the phone off the shaken young woman and tried to calm Tania down. Tania shouted out to her husband, Dave, to get young Kaleb. Thankfully, he was still home. Dave told her not to panic. He was trying hard to stay positive. As they drove the longest twenty minutes of their life, Tania knew in her heart that there was nothing positive about the scene they were about to witness.

The roadblock, flashing lights and drizzling rain only deepened her despair. She leapt from the car and was immediately stopped by a police officer. He forbade her to go further. All the panic and confusion was reflected in the expression on Steve's face; the horror of the accident vivid in his eyes. He had seen the whole event in his rear vision mirror. She hugged him and could feel the pain coursing through his body. In severe shock, he told how he had sat with Tyson until the police arrived. His eyes were wet with unshed tears and all they could do was wait.

A young unlicensed woman had driven the other car but it was clear the accident had been Tyson's fault. He was on the wrong side of the road and she didn't have enough experience to avoid his car. Tania wanted to be with Tyson and asked to travel in the ambulance with him. He was beyond an ambulance and the coroner was taking his body. Tania took Tyson's car that Steve had been driving, and Dave followed behind in their car as they mournfully drove home.

Then came the grim task of identifying their precious son's body. You would expect it to be done in a hospital, in privacy, but Tania and Dave were not given this last moment of time with their son with any of the respect they deserved.

They were met in the car park of the hospital by a police officer and led to a van in an Ambulance bay at the back of the hospital. The doors opened; lying inside was a body bag. The driver of the van pulled the body bag out and unzipped it to reveal their first-born son. As they viewed him, memories and tears rushed by in a flood. Here he was, no dignity, no respect, their whole world shattered in a moment of madness. The road that lay ahead was dim. Dave and Tania would be forever haunted by that moment.

After Tyson died, his partner asked Dave and Tania to look after Kaleb full-time and eventually they were awarded full custody.

Kaleb's health was a big issue and the young woman could not cope. So six weeks after the death of their son, Tania and Dave had to push their grief aside and became surrogate parents for their grandson.

I will always remember the first time I heard Tania's voice on the phone. It was not long after my own mother had died, and I was sitting in front of mum's favourite variety store, thinking about her. Tania had called my private mobile number. I asked her how she got it and she told me she had seen it in the 'Oz Bike' article, which had been published a long time ago. I could sense urgency with this caller and assured her I would give her name to my PA and we would try and push her forward a bit.

I met the whole family a few months later at a show. I walked on the stage that night and immediately fell off, much to my embarrassment and to the delight of the crowd. The second reading of the night had been about a Barry who had died in an accident and had a younger accident victim with him. This reading was claimed but eventually led nowhere.

After the show, Tania, Dave and their daughter, Ashley, approached me and told me how they thought that the Barry reading might have been theirs. I sensed a child in spirit with them and asked them to stay for a bit. I knew he had not long gone and instantly saw tattoos on his arm, which I described to his mother, and also indicated exactly where they stopped. I knew he liked to party and was into marijuana. He made it clear he had passed instantly and was careful with his appearance. He indicated he would like to acknowledge an A name, which turned out to be his sister standing before me. He asked me to tell her how much he loved her. He told me she had a tattoo done in his honour.

Then he showed me a sign that indicated he'd been very fond of underarm deodorant. As strange as it might seem, it had been a phobia for Tyson in his life. I could see there had been some type of disagreement over a car stereo quite recently and that was when Dave walked away in disbelief. It turned out that only two days before, there had been a fight over Tyson's car stereo. Then he acknowledged a little boy who was now two with a K name. That of course was young Kaleb. He told me how the birth had been traumatic. He mentioned his mate, Steve, and then requested that his family do a scrapbook about him for his son to look at later in life. He wanted Steve to put in his memories too. The tears in Tania's eyes told me we had just made a wonderful connection and the look on Dave's face doubly confirmed it.

You would think with a tale this sad that the universe would smile at this brave family in regards to young Kaleb. However, Kaleb's young life is plagued with hospitals and operations as he has Cerebral Palsy.

Since that first meeting at the show, I have had many dealings with Tania, on the phone, at a 'Soul Healing' day, and more recently at one of my retreats. She is a remarkable woman and the best grandmother young Kaleb could ask for. As I am writing this, young Kaleb has just undergone six operations in less than two months.

But there are some good news as well for this strong determined family, as their daughter, Ashley, has just announced her pregnancy. Everyone on the *Spirit Whispers* team prays for young Kaleb almost daily. He is such a beautiful soul and such an amazing teacher despite being only four years old. He has helped heal Tania and Dave's heart, and though each day is a constant battle with his health, his smiling face gives them all the strength they need to keep going. Now, a new baby will be inducted in this most special family. With each new soul born into a family of survivors, all the strength and hope that have been drained as a result of a tragic death are replenished.

Tyson will always be a special spirit. In human form, he inspired and captured the hearts of many. In spirit form, he has added the *Spirit Whispers* team and myself to his many fans. His family have become like my own family. No matter what, we will always be there for each other.

Chapter 18

Not long after the tour with the two mediums ended, I found myself emotionally drained. I had nothing left in me. I was missing my mum like crazy. Every day, I woke up in tears. Despite the constant demand for readings and emails asking for help, I just needed to stop. I had nothing left to give and needed to escape from my world.

I felt like I wanted to crawl into a cave and stay there for a while to just think and lick my wounds. I knew losing mum would be painful but I had put my grief to the side to continue working.

Now it was payback time. I was slipping lower and lower into one of the bluest funks I can remember.

It was around that time that I heard about a silent meditation retreat called 'Vipassana,' which means to see things as they really are. It is one of India's most ancient techniques of meditation. It was taught in India more than 2500 years ago as a remedy for universal ills.

This meditation technique is taught at ten-day residential courses, during which participants learn the basics of the method, and practice sufficiently to experience its beneficial results.

I decided to register for the April retreat.

It was clearly stated that all mobile phones and outside communication would not be tolerated and that there was to be absolutely no speaking. Furthermore, in the interest of the technique, it would be preferred if eye contact was kept at a minimum.

I surrendered my mobile phones after filling out the registration papers and found that on the first afternoon you were able to communicate freely. It was interesting to find some people were doing their 21st retreat. Others were there for the second or third time, and all assured me it was an experience not to be forgotten. I listened eagerly to all the information. To be honest, I was wondering what I had got myself into. Did they really mean no talking whatsoever, or maybe just a little?

We all started the retreat with our first vegetarian meal. There would be nothing but vegetarian meals for the duration of the whole retreat. That suited me, as I had been a vegetarian for about four years. I found that we had our main meal at lunchtime, dinner consisting of a piece of fruit and a cup of tea. I pondered the weight loss I would experience. We were told we were not to over exert ourselves. Some people had thought we could do yoga or any similar practice, but apparently this was taboo. I had intended on keeping doing the Chi Gong I had taken up late the previous year, but apparently not at this retreat.

After a supper of soup, we all sat in the dining hall to be prepped for the following ten days. The men and women would be segregated totally and this started in the prep hall. We were told we could approach the teachers and speak to them, but were encouraged to avoid this if possible. We could not read or write while in the retreat and all intoxicants were banned.

Every time a gong sounded, it was time for either a meal or meditation. There was the opportunity to meditate for up to twelve hours a day, however, it was required you participate for a minimum of six hours. I must admit to thinking this would be easy on the first day!

After the prep, it was time to go to the meditation hall and the silence began. It was surreal in the way everyone immediately stopped talking. When there had been laughter and chatting, now everything was deathly silent. Not a word or even a sigh, and no one would look at anyone, except me!

It was an amazing transformation. Day one started at four thirty am and the meditation did not stop until nine pm. We started the meditation with 'Apana', which means to focus on the breath flowing in and out of the nostrils. I remember sitting there listening to the voice of Mr S.N. Goenka, who is the guiding hand in directing and operating the Vipassana centres around the world. All of the teachings during the ten days are on CD or DVD and this is the only voice you will hear for that duration of the retreat. The trouble was that the man had a very broad Indian accent. I actually thought he was saying, "Breathe in through the nose drills and out through the nose drills." This went on for hours, and there I was, sitting wondering what *nose drills* were! For the first two days, I wasn't even sure I had it right. Nose drills? What could they be? Eventually on day three, I realised he was saying *nostrils*!

I felt totally stupid and with all the silence, I had time to think about this a lot. The pain was beginning to settle in. It is extremely hard to sit still for one-hour sessions. Although you are able to get up and walk around quietly, when you resume the position, the pain quickly slips back into the same areas. I began to focus on the pain instead of the breathing, and by the end of day three was starting to panic. I wanted to go to the hospital and get a shot or something.

You are given a room with three beds, and in this incredibly small place you are expected to cohabit without talking. On day two, one of the roomies decided she could take no more. She was ready to leave, but was convinced otherwise and given a tent.

I broke the most essential rule and asked my remaining roommate if she had paracetamol. She was very upset at this infringement to her silence; she truly wanted to do this with no noise. I told her not to speak and she gave me what she had, however, it seemed to irritate her for the remaining time. Now *I* wanted a tent but decided to stick it out. I was not dealing with it all well. I wanted to shout or something. Painful memories were arising unbidden. It was hard, very hard.

Day four proved to be the most painful, and I am sure I only managed to sit for about four hours. I approached the teachers and asked if I could go to the hospital and they told me the pain would disappear on day five, the day they taught Vipassana.

There was nothing and no one that could convince me a simple meditation would relieve this pain. On the morning of day five, they taught us the new technique. Basically you started at the top of your head and, as if you were a third person, you observed every inch of your body. One inch at time, you moved in a circular motion down the body, right down to the tip of your toes. You were simply to observe, and if there was any pain present, you thought to yourself, 'There is pain here', and then you moved to the next inch. You were to do this up and down the body constantly for the whole day. It worked. When you become the observer of your pain, it arises and then passes away. It is like looking from a distance and not allowing yourself to become emotionally involved in the pain.

After using this technique for the remaining time of the retreat, you are able to see what a useful tool this can be in everyday life. It basically enables you to see that everything in life will be whether you want it to or not. Bad things will happen, such as death and disaster. As much as we wish it away, it has happened. Dwelling on the pain for too long will only create more pain. I found that in the first four days, by dwelling on the pain, it created a mass of pain in my body that felt permanent. However, when we were taught to simply observe it and move to the next area, you soon forgot about the previous pain.

So in life, if we focus on grief or disaster for too long, it becomes permanent. However, if we understand and accept the pain and move forward, it lessens. When we keep going back to it, we relive it. So in order to achieve happiness in this life, we must learn to observe and move forward. This includes the good things as well, because if we constantly live in the moment of a happy time and compare it to other moments, we will not be awake in the present to experience further happy moments. So everything that arises, pain or happiness, must pass. To move forward in a fluid motion, in a state of awareness and observation, will make this life much easier to deal with.

Although I was learning a lot, I spent much of my time observing the other retreat members and this became like a huge mind game. I started to secretly read other members and I knew it was evasion but couldn't help it.

I felt that the segregation was playing havoc with the minds of some of the young men. It became my habit to settle myself in the hall early, especially to watch the watchers. There were some very attractive young ladies there who favoured the exotic retreat wear that quite often revealed more than they may have known. The young men, however, had seen it all and I began to notice that two of them would be settled in their places well before the women, just to watch them snuggle into the meditation posture. I often wonder if they ever had the guts to talk to any of them after the retreat.

Then there was the effect the diet was having on most people, especially the German woman in front of me. I have what I call 'fart humour.' I cannot help myself and will laugh if I hear one go off. The German woman sat there from day three onwards, farting like a backfiring vehicle. I had to suppress my laughter over and over again and kept looking around in case someone else would share my crappy humour.

But a silent retreat is just that, and most of the old students were very serious indeed. It was hard to even fathom what they were like; they were so closed in their own self.

At the retreat was when mum decided to visit me. It was also the place where I became a little unhinged about her death. I let the grief settle for a bit and then I let it go. It was a hard process but the meditation did help me stay in the moment and only drift off on occasions.

By day nine, I had had enough and wanted out. I stuck it out and on day ten, the silence was broken. We were finally able to talk and laugh about our personal experiences. It seemed we all had funny thoughts and tales, and I wasn't the only one who heard the German woman. She was deadly embarrassed!

So at the beginning of the eleventh day, I set off with a car full of people, having offered to give them a lift. I had a strange sense of knowing in my heart. I felt odd and strange, and the outside world hit us like a bomb, such was the noise.

I had found out I could hire a retreat venue on the Gold Coast and began my plan to hold my own retreats in the future. Not silent retreats though, but a longer version of the 'Healing seminar.' The seed was planted and the shoots were rising, but in the meantime, I had a show to do that very day. So after I dropped off the last passenger, I called Debbie. She picked me up and we set off for one of the most memorable shows I have ever conducted.

Chapter 19

The show was a boutique show with only twenty-five or so people in attendance. I felt very light-headed after being in a silent retreat for so many days, and everything seemed a little surreal. I had never felt so calm before a show; it was almost an out-of-body experience. There were, as usual, more women than men in the room, and I began the session by talking about the retreat I had just returned from. This generated a lot of interest as these people usually met weekly for meditation.

I started the readings and began with a woman whose husband was coming through. Detail after detail was validated and then strangely, I felt my mum's spirit around. I questioned it for a moment and then came up with the name Paul or a similar surname. The name was 'Palato' and when I had a closer look at the woman I was reading, I realised she was the wife of my mum's mechanic! I could barely believe I was bringing through the man who had worked on our family cars for many years and my mum was with him. It made me very emotional.

As all good mediums know, it is wise not to get emotional and to move forward. My attention was pulled to a man wearing sunglasses. The sunlight filtered through the window and framed him with a golden glow. He was clearly uncomfortable being in a room with us all but happy enough to have a reading. He had accompanied his mother and his mother-in-law to the show, as his mum wanted a connection with his dad. However, his dad really only wanted to talk to him. The man's name was John and as I started to read, the closeness he and his father enjoyed became very apparent. They had the perfect father-son relationship and at times, the mother had felt quite left out. His father left no stone unturned in the reading, making sure again and again that his son knew how close he was to him, even telling us his spirit rode on the back of John's new motorbike .

John sat there in the afternoon sunlight with tears streaming down his face. Despite his effort to hide his eyes behind sunglasses, a once very sceptical young man walked out changed forever. As a box of tissues was passed around the room, it was clear no one present would be likely to forget that reading.

Eight months later, we found ourselves in the same venue and once again John was there, but this time he was in spirit form. He had died only a month earlier from an aggressive tumour. On his deathbed, he had insisted his wife come to see me, promising he would come through. It became clear why his father had been sticking so close. John was a very easy spirit to read and although his tears had flowed at our last meeting, this time mine did. I broke the sacred medium rule of not falling into emotion. I could barely believe that it was him. There had been no warnings during our previous meeting that he was soon to go home to spirit, but then why would the spirit world want us to know such things? Bad news always comes quickly enough. Why give bad news sooner than necessary? His tumour was aggressive from the start, and for reasons only known to the spirit realm, this time the impending bad news was kept secret. I was happy that he had chosen me to be his medium; it felt like an honour of the highest calibre. It all seemed like an elaborate plan had begun in May to prepare this man for his early demise. He left this life with full knowledge that his father would be there, and that he would also be able to communicate with his family afterwards. The synchronicities of spirit will always amaze me in their timing.

The first reading had taken place in May 2007, and in June, I found myself sinking once again into another depression. It seemed like ends did not want to meet. I was still unhappy at home, with Rebmen and I fighting more than ever. Mum was gone and Debbie was my only release from this lonely life. I felt people were only interested in my gift. I had been single for three years, but was hesitant to look for another relationship. I knew that if I did, Rebmen would be destroyed, despite the fact we were just housemates now and had been for three years. He had not let go of the hope that I would return as his lover. I could only think of him as a brother though. I felt compelled to look out for him and always tried to cheer him up when I was home. I had just returned from a small tour in central Queensland, and although it had been successful, my bills were just piling up.

So the depression was setting in again, and I struggled to stay sane and keep it all together. I was truly sick of it all. I had gained weight and had lost hope of ever being out of debt.

My mum had had enough of my crying and one day, I heard her voice yelling at me from the spirit realms to wake up to myself and get it together. She reminded me of the power of exercise and ordered me to go to a gym and start releasing the grief I felt from her death and the negative energy that was storing up. Finally I listened. After all, it was mum, and I had craved to hear her voice so much that when she finally did speak, I went straight downtown and joined the first gym I found. The first day of exercise found me sweating like a pig and hating every minute of it. But once again, after it was all over, my body started to respond to the positive actions and I finally exhaled after a terribly exhausting six months.

It did not take long for the positive effects of exercise to weave its magic. Once again, I found myself feeling positive and planning a new tactic to survive the financial side of the business. I decided to start doing low-priced monthly shows in venues around Brisbane as my friend, Ezio De Angelis, did in Sydney. I hoped it would help alleviate the high expense of travel, as well as giving my regular patrons a chance to catch up with me monthly and witness the wonderful world of spirit again and again.

I felt I had finally found a winner and it truly was a pleasure to only have to travel an hour or so to a venue, rather than having to take a cut lunch, a waterbag and three planes just to do a show! The numbers were not over the top, but in each show the validations kept getting stronger and more awe-inspiring. With each show came a fresh batch of newly bereaved people grasping for answers. Some left disappointed, some elated, but all left wanting to know more about the mystical world of spirit.

It was also time to make positive changes in my home life and finally in September 2007, I found my own home and moved away from Rebmen. I still loved him as my dearest friend but his depression and false hope in getting back with me could not continue. I moved to a rather noisy place but for the first time in a while, I felt free.

The old house had held many memories for me, good and bad. It was where my development had taken place and more recently where my dog, Jessie, and my cat, Biddy, had disappeared. All the psychic powers in the world gave me no clue to where they might be. It was horrible, as I loved them both dearly. I called them for months, rang the pound and the vets, but there was never a sign of either of them again.

Chapter 20

One of the first shows we conducted in our monthly round was in September.

As Deb and I cruised down the highway to the Redlands Sporting Club, I felt a spirit jump into the car. He was amazingly clear, telling me his name was Daniel. I mistakenly thought it might be the Daniel whose family I had been helping through their grief, and questioned Deb to see if she knew they were coming. She didn't know but remarked it seemed strange as this was not their area, but there was no doubt in my mind. The boy's name was Daniel. He had red hair and had passed in an accident. There could not have been too many like him, surely?

It was not long into the show when young Daniel made his presence known again. It all came back during the reading. I had met this spirit before but he was not the one I thought. This boy was from a family who had had more than their share of grief.

Wendy was the mother of this forward young spirit, and had also given birth to seven other children. One of them hadn't made it past birth, a little girl named Angela who never drew her first breath. This had happened almost twenty years earlier, at a time when mediums were not common, and death was a part of life you had to deal with whether you wanted to or not.

In January 2006, Wendy was driving past the John Tonge Centre (the morgue at Coopers Plains, Brisbane) when she felt a sickening heart-dropping sensation in the pit of her stomach. Fear engulfed her for the remainder of the drive as a voice in her head told her she would be visiting that centre very soon. She shook the feeling away and tucked the fear in the back of her mind, telling herself it was nothing.

A few days later, her 22-year-old son, Ben, dropped by in very high spirits to repay a loan to his grandmother. He teased and joked with his family, yelling endearments from the bottom of the stairs before he left and went on his way. His mother was glad to see him smile again. In November the previous year, a motorcycle accident had made him deeply depressed and unable to work due to no vehicle and no money. He lived with his girlfriend and they had been fighting a lot. On top of it all, he was finding it hard to cope without his drugs.

Ben had always been a happy kid until about 17 years of age, when he started to dabble in marijuana, which eventually progressed to heavier substances and eventually amphetamines. His mum was aware of his habit but kept it secret from his dad. She was well aware that part of his depression stemmed from not having the money to purchase drugs. Sandy had no illusions about her boy but loved him as much as all her children. Sure, she wished he was clean and sober, but she knew that for a time this was just wishful thinking. The amphetamines had changed her son from a sweet, easygoing boy to an empty-shelled haunted man. As a mother, Wendy could only watch from a distance and pray he saw the light. Nothing prepared her for the complete personality change her son experienced. No one warned her nor did she have any easy access to information on the dangers of this drug. Like a lot of mothers who watch their children deteriorate from drugs, she had no idea that this drug was akin to holding a loaded gun to your head and playing Russian roulette. She thought you could only die from heroin. No one told her that amphetamines could kill.

The problem with amphetamines is that it is not the actual drug that kills you, but the side effects of the drug. Clinical depression caused by lack of sleep, paranoia, poor diet and complete tunnel vision can contribute to one of the worst deaths any parent can face: suicide.

Unknown to Wendy or even Ben, that sunny day in January would be the last time she would see her son smile. The news arrived by phone just as she and her husband sat down for dinner. Ben had committed suicide by hanging himself.

It was Kat, Ben's girlfriend, who had found him. She was now on the phone crying the bad news through the phone lines.

Wendy was immediately in absolute shock. She screamed at Kat to resuscitate Ben, but Kat kept screaming that he was dead. Wendy was distraught when a male police officer took the phone and tried to calm her down. It was too late for first aid.

She and her husband travelled the longest 20 km they had ever travelled. The silence was like a dark heavy energy consuming the occupants of the vehicle with fear and desperation, deep and unforgiving. They arrived at Ben's house to find the coroner already on the scene. It was over. The spirit world had claimed another child. Her other son, Andrew, who was meant to be on the other side of town also pulled in the driveway. He was hysterical. He was meant to be out with friends but some instinct or maybe Ben's spirit had told him to be there. Ben had passed away at 3pm that afternoon. It was now 5pm.

A week after her drive past the morgue with a sickening feeling in the pit of her stomach, she found herself at the gates of the John Tonge centre, but this time she didn't drive past. She drove in with her family and parked the car. She was led to a small room where a kind woman prepared them for the sight they were about to see. Eventually, they were led through another door, which led to a cold and sparsely furnished room. In the middle of that room was a bed, and on that bed was her son. There were no warm smiles this time.

The funeral came and went. The slow path of grief arose before them like a cavernous black mountain with treacherous slopes waiting to be scaled. Suicide deaths are different from any other deaths. The questions and the feelings of inadequacy balloon out of proportion as everyone affected by the death spends time in their own thoughts, trying to grasp a feasible answer to their role in the death. Everyone has a different take on the situation; some blame themselves, others get angry, and some even contemplate taking their own life. In accidents or illnesses, it is fate or the hand of God, whichever way you prefer to see it. But with suicide, it is chosen by someone you thought you knew, someone you thought was upfront with you, someone you would have moved Heaven and Earth to help, someone who didn't think about your feelings before they left.

The remaining children of this family all grieved in different ways, as usually happens in family units. Jamie and Daniel felt let down, as Ben had been their idol. Jamie took it exceptionally hard. Andrew seemed to find spiritual solace and became even more intuitive. He is to this day. Tony, Rene and Jasmine all went on anti-depressants and Jasmine (a speed user at the time) became deeply distressed. She had spent many hours with Ben indulging in their addiction. The father of this large family found it hard to understand 'why' his son took his own life. But he tried very hard to support the whole family, all the while fighting his own demons. Ben's torment had ended but the family's hell had just begun. Guilt, fear and loss consumed them all. Through it all, Wendy strived to hold her brood together, always staying upbeat and positive despite the constant ache in her heart. She was the essential glue and without her, who knows what would have happened to the rest of them?

After Ben died, Wendy made an appointment to see me with a couple of her children. Ben came straight through and did not hold back. All the details of his death were given, and although I cannot remember the reading now, Wendy told me that this reading saved her very soul. It gave her validation Ben was still with them in spirit and the reading prevented her from going over the edge.

You would like to think this would be the end of this family's pain. However, the black mountain was to grow larger and more treacherous, with slippery slopes becoming even more hazardous.

Chapter 21

Only 15 months later, in the predawn hours of a Sunday morning, Wendy and Jeff were woken up by spotlights flooding their lounge room. A heavy knocking reverberated through the house and when the door opened, a policeman was standing on their front door step. Wendy's heart sank and she began to tremble with a sickening apprehension.

This time it was Daniel. The spirit world had claimed a third child.

A silent scream echoed throughout the house, as the details of his death were revealed by this stranger in uniform, a stranger who wished he had not just witnessed a young boy in the stillness of death.

Daniel, their over-the-top cheeky redheaded son, had been drinking when he decided he needed cigarettes. He took off on his motorbike to go to the service station. A little too drunk, a little too cocky, Daniel hit a tree and died on impact only a thousand metres from the place where Ben ended his own life.

Wendy collapsed on the lounge, a numbness taking over her entire being. Once again they had to visit the John Tonge centre, and again they were led to the room where the dead are displayed for formal identification. All the way to the morgue, Wendy prayed this one had been a mistake, but all wisps of hope disappeared with one look. There was no mistake. There were no exits; it was straight to hell again.

The family was only just coming to terms with Ben's death and Wendy was worried about all of them. How would they cope? Wendy and Daniel had been so close and he had still been living at home. He was a noisy, active boy and now the silence was deafening. The house seemed empty and colourless.

There was another funeral, brimming with hundreds of mourners. Everyone in their local area came to pay their respects, purely out of compassion for a family who had more than their fair share.

Their life was falling apart. Jeff had taken to sleeping in Daniel's room and although quietness lurked in the corners of their house, Wendy could swear her cheeky red-haired boy was still following her. Once again, Wendy approached me for a reading. This one was by phone.

Daniel came through wearing a cowboy hat and proclaiming his love for country and western music. I had found this strange for an 18 year-old city boy. He told me no one was to blame. It was an accident. He proudly showed me his unruly mop of red hair and then brought forward his brother and sister, Ben and Angela. He told me he had loved his life and had lived it to the fullest. Most importantly, he was okay and happy with his spirit siblings. He assured his mum that they were all okay. Once again, Wendy was given some much needed relief from the reading and has since told me that without them, she may not have fared as well as she has.

Love carried on from the spirit world with all of this brave lady's children appearing in front of me. They made sure they gave messages for their mum in a show full of people, despite the fact she had had previous readings. She had managed to stay off anti-depressants or any other intoxicants, legal or otherwise. I asked her how she coped and she told me that she spent her time honouring her children in different ways. She told me that love in the family is what she had pushed for, and that they had pulled together knowing their children were still around in spirit, walking by their side.

She has taken up creating a scrapbook and has also made a quilt out of her sons' clothing. She is not sure she will ever heal entirely, but she needs to be strong for the rest of her family. Her husband doesn't do so well and lives with a large burden of grief. Wendy has been sent to this family as a pillar of strength to help them through these harsh lessons of death.

She has also lost a mum and a sister, Debbie, who passed at only 26 years of age from cancer. I feel Wendy is going amazingly well and this is the reason why I wished to honour her in this book.

So many people fall apart when death strikes. Although it is a natural event, we all need someone to support the weaker of us. I was lucky in my life to have my mum prop me up through the deaths of my brother and daughter. Wendy is made of stern stuff, much like my mum, and I feel she has got it. She told me that she doesn't dwell on the past and stays in the present. She is now a proud grandmother of three and has seen most of her remaining children pull together since the horrific period, which altered their lives forever. Babies and weddings now colour their once grey lives. In my eyes, Wendy should be proud of her strength and can truly be an example for many of you reading this book.

She is a living proof that rolling up your sleeves and getting on with it can be the key to surviving the grief of losing a child. She unselfishly allowed her family to fall apart and quietly propped them up one by one, with barely a thought for herself. All too often, I hear women and men complain that their husband or wife is not supporting them, that they are consumed by their own grief and have stopped being the parent and partner they promised to be. They indulge in sadness for way too long while the rest of their family slowly disintegrates, and when all is lost, they cry about the new losses in their life.

It is our human right to grieve, however, it is not wise or fair to dwell and bathe in the grief. Wendy's strength has enabled her children to go on having normal lives, to overcome their grief and to move forward. I have found that in the many families who come to me in such sad situations, there is always one who strives to be the pillar. If that person is you, thank you for being strong. If that person is another family member, then you need to acknowledge their strength and their gift of selflessness. You need to thank them. If we can all work together as a family unit in this world we will find we have everything we need.

Chapter 22

Despite the sadness of having to leave my home, it felt like my life was refreshed in my very own place. When I left, I left it clean. It stayed that way and there was no heavy air of depression permanently fermenting the house. I didn't realise how much these things had adversely affected me until they were removed. I began to think clearly, my readings improved and my weight started to drop. I didn't even know I had been 'comfort eating' until then. I still spoke to Rebmen daily and we quite often went places together, but in my mind we had finally broken the hope he once held.

With less stress and more time to relax, I read more books and became fascinated with hypnotherapy. I devoured books by Michael Newton and Brian Weiss about their work with past lives and life-between-life regressions. I felt I had found a key. Every time a mother wept in a show or private reading, I felt a longing to give her more, which grew and flourished into a raging passion. I thought constantly how great it would be to group these women together and teach them all that spirit had taught me. I had been doing one-day workshops for parents but there was never enough time to teach all I had discovered. My mind kept flitting back to the retreat I had done in May and how it had benefited me. I researched all the possibilities and finally found a retreat that was economically priced. I planned and thought of all we could do in two days.

The work of Michael Newton and Brian Weiss bubbled and frothed in my mind. One day, I decided I was going to try hypnosis for a past-life and 'life-between-lives' regression. I found a man named Peter Smith in Melbourne who was Australia's representative for the Michael Newton Institute. I called him and told him what I did. Once again, I found myself booking a plane to Melbourne, this time in search of answers in an effort to help bereaved parents gain more information to help alleviate their grief.

As the plane touched down, all I could feel was a queer sense of apprehension. I was scheduled to meet Peter, and the prospect of being regressed back into my past life, while intriguing, was still slightly intimidating. What if I was a bad person in my past life? Did I really want to know?

Peter arrived to pick me up from my hotel in the middle of a thunderstorm. He was a slim man, casually dressed and softly spoken and as I found out on the drive to his office, incredibly passionate about his work. He seemed to be quite empathetic and compassionate as we talked. It was with all reservations gone that I handed him my list of 'people to find' in my past lives, with the goal of understanding their roles in both my past lives and my current life.

The storm raged outside as Peter lulled me into hypnosis, the crackling and booming a thousand miles away, as his soothing voice sent me travelling backward through time. Happy memories and landmark occasions in my life flew by, as Peter encouraged me to go deeper and deeper, his urgings almost in time with the claps of thunder in the real world I was quickly melting away from. I even went back to the womb, experiencing and reliving my impressions of life before birth, suddenly becoming aware of my mother's anxieties at the time, her worries about Dad, her distrust.

And then I started visiting my previous lives.

The first life I visited ended almost two centuries ago, in 1815. I was a man named Russel, a chronic drinker and a widower, who lived in Holland. He had died of liver disease. My wife, Aline, had died very young of an unspecified illness, which seemed fitting in a morbid way, when I realised she'd been that life's incarnation of my late daughter Crystal. When she'd died, I'd become incredibly bitter, and took up heavy drinking with my best friend Wilhelm. I had pushed away my only son (an incarnation of my oldest son, Alan), who subsequently died young as well, never seeing me again.

All in all, it seemed like the most terrible path my current life could have taken if I'd succumbed to the alcohol or drugs. This proved to be no coincidence. After leading a terrible life in Holland (during my life-between-lives as 'Minna') I'd come to the conclusion that I'd inflicted some terrible wrongs in that life, and would rectify them in the next. My soul group helped me, pushing me to learn some hard lessons I never had as Russel.

For instance, Crystal –Aline in my last life– died much earlier in this life, but from the unique and much more painful position as my daughter. As a result, her death was much harder, and a much bigger obstacle to overcome, but somehow I did. Even though I took the same road as I did hundreds of years ago by embracing alcohol, I learnt from others this time. I took the path less travelled to a more healthy recovery from grief. When I drove my son, Alan, away because of my drug use, to a new and somewhat healthier life with his Dad, I fought hard to win back his love instead of again wallowing in self-pity and amphetamines. I had truly been given the option of giving up and wallowing in substance abuse twice, even being presented with the same drinking and drug buddy (Wilhelm in this life presented himself as my ex-partner Rebmen) but I turned it down both times.

Maybe I was learning something this time?

Another life I visited was much earlier, in the 12th century in Italy. I seemed to visit near the end of that life, stepping out of this world and back in time to the life, my life, of an old and haggard woman. I seemed to be a cleaner, and lit the church candles near where I lived. I hated the priest who was stationed there with a vile passion. The priest was someone I knew quite well in this life. He had incarnated in that life as the priest and had sexually assaulted me repeatedly, soiling me at a time and place that valued virginity so much.

Regardless, as a crippled old woman in 12th century Italy, I did not have this spiritual perspective. His rape had stopped all other men from wanting to marry me, and I'd grown old and bitter, hating the priest who did this to me and slowly, over time, extending that hatred to men as a whole. I'd become a lonely, angry old woman who felt that men were just pigs who lived to please themselves at the expense of others, especially me. It was depressing.

After this tragic glimpse of the 12th century, I was treated to a more hopeful vision of the other side in my life-between-lives as the soul, Minna. Apparently, I am doing well in the grand scheme of things. On the other side, I'm about to go up a level after the experiences I've suffered and learned from in this life. My daughter, Crystal, is still leagues ahead of me in terms of 'spirit evolution', but is still a part of my soul group regardless. Like many souls, she also prefers shorter lives that teach powerful lessons to her peers. Also, perhaps predictably, in stark contrast with my guide, Peter, who can be very strict, I have a very playful and lazy soul which doesn't like to incarnate very often.

As Minna, I was also given a rare glimpse of the spirit world. I found myself disembodied, and saw igloo-shaped domes. One was very green and had thousands of trees in it. I felt it was Earth or a gateway to Earth for those beginning new lives. The other one was very much like a library filled with thousands of bookcases and tens of thousands of books. I was asked by someone to go to a book, any book, and find the meaning of life. The first book I chose out of every book there said three words: 'alchemy and gold.' I took it to mean I needed to be magical in this life and evolve to level gold in the spirit world. But from my limited earthbound perspective, I can never be sure.

I was told I have lived 46 lives throughout my long experience: 19 as a woman and 27 as a man. Clearly, I prefer the life of a man. side seems to be consistent throughout all my lives, and I on't enjoy being directed and ordered around by men as a woman, but I seem to take on female lives for the dual purposes of learning lessons impossible to learn as a man, and balancing out my soul evolution. I also take on addictive lives more often than not!

The final interesting thing that came out of the experience was that I was told that in six months time, I was going to be on television…and lose some weight! I took the second piece of information more seriously than the first.

Six months later, I was filming 'The One', and the entire experience was suddenly validated for me. If this simple little prediction was correct, then surely the sum total of the experience was truthful as well. Knowing that one's life does have a preordained purpose, and that I was fulfilling mine reasonably well, felt really good.

As Peter dropped me off at the airport, my mind was abuzz. All I could think about was how I could pass on the messages and information I had learned to my clients. As the plane flew higher and higher into the clouds, I realised the only way to spread this hopeful message was to write a book.

Chapter 23

The treatment had given me more than I could have hoped for. It validated everything I had previously thought and been told. In my early days of training as a medium, my friend Jane suggested I was responsible for choosing my own life. I told her she was nuts. Why would I choose a life filled with such tragedy? Surely I would choose to be rich? She just smiled and told me to think about it. Naturally the thought swirled around my mind for days and I started to discuss the subject with my guide. He confirmed what she had said.

Peter, my guide, explained to me that life was like a school and we all have certain lessons we have agreed to complete in our current physical incarnation. He told me I had chosen this life and all the people around me. My mother, father, daughter, sons, siblings and friends were all hand chosen to assist in learning the lessons I have agreed to. My family and friends have chosen me for the same reason. These people are members of my soul group and because of our personal level of advancement in the spirit realms we consistently incarnate together. We also switch roles in order to increase our learning capacity. In the last life, I was my daughter's husband, in this life I was her mother, in the next I may be her brother. Whatever role we choose to play will be carefully considered to benefit the well-being and the advancement of all souls involved. We also choose our human bodies to suit the life and lessons we wish to learn. Some souls choose to incarnate into disabled or handicapped bodies. This will teach their loved ones some very important lessons. The disabled person will advance and learn much from taking on this type of life and all the frustrations that accompany it.

I have gained a lot by reading the books written by Dr Michael Newton. In his book *Journey of the Soul* he found that by hypnotising subjects and regressing them back beyond their current life, he was able to access their previous lives. He found he was able to take his subjects to the point of death, and then to what happens after death has occurred. Not only was he accessing our past lives but also our life-between-lives. He discovered he could talk to his subjects' souls while still in the spirit realm.

Michael found this realm to be a highly organised place. A lot of preparation is put into choosing a life for every soul. Every soul has a guide and is part of a soul group or cluster. Every soul interacts with members of their soul group and also with secondary soul groups.

His work does not suggest that the realm has punishment, however, each soul is aware of what it should be doing and spends time reviewing each past life before considering future ones. If a past life has been deemed unsuccessful, this will be taken into consideration and efforts will be made to balance any karmic debts. So if you killed someone, this will need to be balanced out. Not necessarily by being killed by the same person, but you may choose to be a doctor who saves the future life of the soul you killed in a previous life. If you hurt people by displaying aggressive and hateful behaviour, you may have to be a victim of the same behaviour in a future life to understand how it felt. Ultimately, every soul has a level they are working at and a higher level they are working toward. Some will proceed in their quest for perfection quickly, while others may have to keep working on the same type of lives and lessons for many incarnations.

When I first read Michael's book, I was very excited. Everything in it correlated with what my guides had already said. They had told me about reincarnation and the soul journey, and I knew deeply that what they were saying was true. It was the only thing that made sense of Life. Now that I've had the treatment, I am certain that it can help ease the grief felt by many of you reading these words.

Our souls are eternal and forever advancing to a state of perfection, and ultimately to a point where we can assist other souls in their journey. When we incarnate, we have already decided on the lessons we wish to learn. To advance our soul, we must learn the lessons of forgiveness, compassion, empathy and unconditional love, just to name a few.

To facilitate a learning environment, we create dramas with members of our soul group to ensure that the lessons are taught. Each life is our own personal movie in which all of our family members, friends and foes play important parts. For instance, my daughter lived for four years but in that time and thereafter she has taught me more lessons than any other member of my soul group. I now view her as an advanced soul who was my greatest teacher.

When she was born, she taught me responsibility and unconditional love. All parents learn this lesson when their child is born. When she was alive, the lesson of selfishness was mine to integrate. I failed in this task at that time. When she died, I was taught the lesson of grief and from that lesson stemmed the negative lessons of anger, revenge and hatred. All of these were mine to overcome and grow from. For years, I let these emotions hold me down but eventually I took responsibility for my actions and choices. I learned the lesson of forgiveness and judgement when I forgave myself and others I felt had treated me unfairly in my life. From her death, I learned compassion and empathy for others in the same situation as me. The lessons I failed with my daughter were given to me again with my sons. I again failed selfishness. Indulging in drugs is a very selfish act, so once again the universe was harsh and my boys were taken away from me. I have finally learned that lesson by overcoming addiction, and now find it easy to put others before myself.

Not only has Crystal taught me, but also through me, she still continues to teach everyone who reads this book and takes something from it. I can now say that my life was planned to be a medium from the spirit realms. I chose to help alleviate the fear of death and teach people how to deal with grief. People and events have been placed strategically throughout my life as signposts to the right direction. Choices were given to make the path hard or easy but both led to the same point.

My spirit guide has been with me from the beginning of time and we are partners in whichever life I choose. When I plan a life, he is always there to make sure that I am choosing wisely, and as I live my life, he is there to steer me back onto the right path should I take a wrong turn. It is his role in my soul contract. In this life, I have open communication with him because of my work as a medium, but I am sure it has not always been so with every incarnation.

I have a friend named Jost Sauer who wrote a book called *Higher and Higher*. In traditional Western methods, drug users are given prescription drugs to wean them off the street drugs. In other words, they fight drugs with drugs. Jost has developed an effective process utilising traditional Chinese medicine, supplements, meditation and exercise to effectively enable heavy drug users to become drug free naturally.

In my view, Jost designed his life from the spirit realms to assist him in reaching his goal. He was born in Germany in the late fifties, well before drug use escalated to the multi billion-dollar industry it has become. His parents were very straight-laced and he incarnated into a rebellious human being. In the early seventies, he immersed himself in drugs of all descriptions and the culture surrounding them. He became an addict for approximately twenty years. There were many hardships that deterred him from freeing himself. Eventually, he developed his own system to remain clean that he now teaches to addicts and other practitioners.

It is clear to me that Jost needed to live the life of an addict before he could help them. His deep-seated beliefs in Eastern philosophies point to a past life spent in that region. His desire to teach and assist others in remaining drug-free tells me he would be a fairly advanced soul. It was as if he and his guide realised there would be a need for this type of therapy long before it was physically apparent. Thus they set about creating the perfect life for Jost to not only understand how drugs affected his own system, but also how they affected his mind. This first-hand knowledge enabled him to create a very effective treatment for addicts everywhere.

Not everyone chooses the life of a medium or spiritual teacher. However, the vast majority choose lives that will add to and bring happiness or nurturing to our fellow human beings. Builders build houses to bring shelter, hairdressers use their skills to make us feel better and musicians create music to make our hearts soar. Mothers raise their children, and farmers raise crops or animals to feed the masses. From the humble factory worker to the most respected doctor, we all work together to assist each other. Many souls have been born to bring awareness to the damage we have been doing to our planet and animals, and they are succeeding. The late Steve Irwin has created a dynasty in that area which will be carried out for many years to come.

Unfortunately, not all souls succeed in their personal life quests and many run off the rails. They are so absorbed by the physical trappings of this world that they become bad and cause many others much pain. Although some may not succeed in this life, they are not judged in the realms by any spiritual court. The judge they face is their own conscience.

Chapter 24

As 2007 drew to a close, I felt more settled than I had in a long while. I was happy in my new home and had managed to get my finances on a much better track. I had a new neighbour who was happy to look after my two dogs, George and Trixie, should I go away. Rebmen and I were still on good terms. As usual, I spent Christmas without my sons as I had done since 1999 and spent some time grumbling about that, but was welcomed at Debbie's house with her family. I still had a lot of past debt, but the monthly shows were becoming successful and word of mouth was spreading. I welcomed 2008 in with Rebmen and anticipated a great new year ahead. Rebmen did seem okay with our friendship by then, and we still spoke on the phone at least once a day. He attended a lot of shows and the ones he couldn't, he always called to wish me luck.

This 'good luck ritual' had started with mum and it ran like this: "Good Luck, not that you need it! 313! Hope you got your lucky knickers on! Have fun!"

When mum died, Rebmen took over and he always remembered to ring and somehow it made me feel secure that the show was going to be fantastic. He truly was my best friend. He and Deb were both truly close to me and I had relied heavily upon them both, especially since mum passed away. Of course, they were no replacement for mum - no one could or would ever be - but they sure helped to get me through that first year. For that, I will be eternally grateful.

I still went to mum's house every school holidays to spend time with my stepfather, brother and my niece Kathleen. My brother would not let us touch mum's room, so in a surreal way it still felt like she might be in there. Sadly she was not. However, I would spend time going through her things and feeling her there because, try as I might, I could not materialise her or even hear her voice. Mediums cannot read for themselves in relation to their spirits. It becomes a case of: "Is this real, is that mum talking or is this just wishful thinking?" If a stranger gives the information you crave, then it becomes validated. If you simply feel like you hear it, you question it.

As 2008 yawned and woke up, I purchased a camcorder to start uploading some of my readings on YouTube. I thought this was what the life-between-lives treatment had meant when the television comment came up. I also purchased a small PA system.

We began the year with a bang. Rebmen was the camcorder man, Debbie running the microphone and me at the front doing what I do best, producing validation after validation. We had a lot of tissue moments. I remember once standing at the front, bringing through a young boy named Connor who had passed at the age of three due to cancer, completely oblivious to everyone except the boy's mother. When for a moment I paused and looked up, all I could see was a box of tissues being passed around the rows.

Then there was a woman who had lost two granddaughters in the same tragedy. They had been in a car trying to cross a flooded road, but had been washed away. Both drowned. What some people were facing was terrible. People had inconceivable tragedies colour their lives on a daily basis. Show after show, we also had some jaw-dropping comments that would make us keel over with laughter.

I will never forget the lady who sat in the front row and asked 'that' question. She wanted to know if spirits were capable of having sex with a living person. As I grappled around my mind for a suitable answer, she went on: "Since my husband died, he has been coming back every night and made love to me. I have to say he is much better at it than he was when he was alive." As my mouth opened and shut like a goldfish, Debbie nearly dropped the microphone. Rebmen almost toppled over the camcorder and you could have heard a pin drop on the carpet as she continued, unashamed and almost boasting: "No, I don't need one of those sex shops. I get all the loving I want for free." The room erupted into laughter and I could only nod stupidly. What will be will be!

I was also doing more one-day seminars helping people deal with their grief, but was finding there was not enough time to cover all subjects. Once again, the retreat idea began to grow and I approached the Theosophical Society about their retreat at Springbrook on the Gold Coast hinterland. We set the first retreat to start mid-March but in the meantime, I had a trip to Queenstown, New Zealand.

I took my son Jack with me and set off over the sea with apprehension. I had booked a venue to do a show and it had not attracted much interest. As the plane taxied down the runway, I knew only two tickets had sold and disappointment hung heavy in my heart.

We were met at the Queenstown airport by one of the most colourful women I have ever met. She had multi-coloured dreadlocks hanging to her waist and a broad Scottish accent. Her name was Sunny Sky and the beauty in her heart penetrated the air around her like a fresh breeze straight from Heaven. I immediately felt comfortable with this exquisite looking woman. It was like I already knew her.

We drove to the town in her jeep and my breath was taken by the views. I fell in love with this town on sight. All my previous fears of poor show numbers were overridden by the beauty and magic of the place. I no longer cared. Sunny took me to her home, which in itself was a wonder. I had never seen such an unusual home. I was then taken to my accommodation for the next few days, the 'Reavers Lodge.' This was a backpackers hostel, however, Jack and I were treated to the best room in the place: a two bedroom self-contained unit. The owner was a beautiful Maori man named Josh who also adorned long dreadlocks. However, his were dark. It was becoming a very spiritual day for me as I felt that I had also met Josh somewhere. My memory strained to recall past lifetimes to no avail. There was no need for absolute validation as the knowing was enough.

The Saturday of the show came way too quickly and only ten people had purchased a ticket. The accuracy of the validations however, made it a memorable show. The venue was framed with the most amazing large window overlooking the mountains. I will never forget it. Josh took us around afterwards and we bought the biggest hamburger Jack had ever eaten at a shop called 'Furburgers.' We ended up having one of the best nights I can remember. The atmosphere of this town filled with people of nationalities from the world over is hard to ignore. It is like being at a festival. Fun filled the night sky and snuck into my heart despite myself.

The next morning, I was on the phone and I turned around as I felt a strong energy directly behind me. There was nothing there but I had the strongest sense of déjà vu I have ever experienced. It came into my body with a strength that took my breath away completely, such was the sense of having 'been here and done this.' I knew I had been here before. I knew I had just experienced a LBL (life-between-lives) recollection.

The theory is that in our LBL or spirit world, we are often shown signposts of our future life to let us know we are on the right track, and for us to look out because life as we know it is about to change abruptly. At that moment, the weirdness took me by surprise and I have never been able to shake it from my mind. I put my heart and soul on alert.

As our weekend in New Zealand came to a close and I hugged my new friends goodbye, I knew that this trip to Queenstown was more than just a show. It signified a complete life change and nothing would shake this belief. I could feel excitement welling up inside of me already. The future beckoned me with alluring fingers and I was more ready than ever.

Chapter 25

When I arrived home, I tried to settle back in my normal routine but was feeling restless. I felt waves of loneliness wash over me. I had been without a partner for almost four years and despite Rebmen constantly wishing me back, I could only think of him as a friend, almost brother-like. I sat staring moodily down the backyard, considering my prospects for a partner. I had recently joined up with an Internet dating company called RSVP. I had not been happy with the results, frequently got hit on by less than scrupulous men, so I had taken my profile down. At about that moment, caught deep in thought, I spied a kingfisher on the back fence. His brilliant blue feathers were iridescent in the sun. He was just looking at me. I had never seen one this close before.

I watched him a little longer and made the decision to have one last look on that damn dating site. I cruised down the first page of men most eligible to me and decided to stuff the romance; I would look for a musician. After all, it was all about filling a spot and sometimes music and love equated. About four rows down on the screen, was a man sitting on a Harley. He looked normal enough. I read his profile and saw he was indeed a talented musician. He could play several instruments and was looking for someone who could sing and perhaps play an instrument. Well, that was me! I was no Celine Dion, but I could hold a rough tune and I still played around with my guitar at times. He also said he worked away in New Guinea most of the time. This was perfect! My life involved a lot of travel and someone like this Patrick person would understand. I immediately put my profile back up and emailed him. I told him I was only going to be on for a short while as I hated being hit on by some of the men on the site. So I sat and waited impatiently.

I looked out the back and noticed the Kingfisher was still there. How odd! I checked my inbox and there was a message from Patrick. He told me he was currently in America visiting his parents. I never realised he was American. He told me he would be back in Australia in a few days. Not good enough! I bossily asked him for his number and told him I would call right now. He obediently sent it and I called him immediately. I think he was a little stunned. We started to chat about the dating site, and I told him I really wanted to just play music with someone. He was happy with that idea and then the strangeness began. I mentioned that my dad had been a musician for twenty-five years to which he responded unenthusiastically. I continued on telling him that dad was a big fat man with only one leg. I heard him take his breath as he yelled: "Stop!"

He asked me if my father's name was Mike Conte. My father's name was really Michael Contarino, but he went under the name of Mike Conte for his work. I almost screamed when I realised this strange man talking to me from America knew my late father. He explained that he had lived in Rockhampton from 1986 onwards. He had met my father there and had played drums in his band occasionally when dad was short of a drummer. I could barely believe it! It really was surreal. I hadn't had much to do with dad after Crystal died, neither when Alan and Jack were born in 1989 and 1994. Patrick had not heard of me at all from dad, but had met my sister, Ellen, who lived with dad for a period of time in Rockhampton.

I really had to meet this man in person now. It seemed as if we were destined to meet. We agreed to meet a few days later when he returned home from his overseas trip. When I got off the phone, I realised it was my spirit brother Martin's birthday. We arranged to meet the following Sunday. It was now a Monday. So I went about my normal business. I went to the gym every day, did readings and was busy organising a small tour of north Queensland and also northern New South Wales.

Every morning, I noticed the kingfisher was still on the fence. He was there every afternoon. It was bugging me. I have a very good friend Scott Alexandra King who specialises in Animal meanings and has written a book called *Animal Dreaming*, so I called him and asked him what it meant. He told me it basically meant that everything was getting ready, and that in two weeks my life would be changed. I now take his book wherever I go, as it has been an essential tool for interpreting messages from the spirit world.

I had no idea how prolific the message from the kingfisher would be. I met with Patrick as arranged, and as I approached his house I noticed a huge kingfisher painted on the fence. The street before his was Kingfisher Street. I did not need any further prompting from the spirit realm, or animal realm for that matter. This meeting was definitely destiny.

I liked Patrick as soon as I met him. I had taken my guitar so I played him some tunes; we talked for a little and then went for a ride on the biggest Harley I had ever seen. He really did seem to be a nice guy. We talked well into the night and I agreed to come back the next night for more chatting. He only had a few days before leaving for his work in New Guinea. He never went to New Guinea though. There was a problem with his visa, so he had to work in Brisbane until it was sorted.

In the meantime, I had my first retreat to organise. It was going to be held at Springbrook and I had sold fifteen tickets. We were holding this event for two days and had secured a wonderful vegetarian cook. The venue is owned by the Theosophical Society, and they have precise guidelines about what can and cannot be done on their premises. Eating meat was forbidden, as was killing animals, drinking, smoking and using illicit drugs. I arrived at the retreat on the Friday afternoon and was blown away by the beauty of the location. It was far more scenic then I could have hoped for. The mountain air literally took my breath away. The cabins were well equipped and when I walked into the dining room to meet the cook, Margaret, my senses were overtaken again, this time by the fragrant smells coming from the kitchen - I was in heaven! I had been a vegetarian for the past five years, but nothing I cooked ever smelt this good. I was instantly in love with Margaret, this wonderful cook. She also had her husband, Mark, helping and her small daughter, Mookie. I had my son Jack with me, and he immediately took a shine to this family and fit right in, hiring himself on as 'dish pig.'

One by one, the retreat participants turned up. Although I knew some of them, I was meeting others for the first time. We had mainly people who had lost children. We also had a lovely Vietnamese man who had lost his wife, and another young man who had lost his girlfriend. These two connected quickly and I was in awe at seeing this mixed group blend so beautifully.

The first night, we gathered in the meeting room and just talked about everything we were to do in the next two days. We did a night meditation, went back to the dining room and had tea before bed. The next day was the tough one: teaching forgiveness, life lessons and acceptance. I had to counteract each 'but' and 'what if' with an answer channelled from my guides. It seemed that in this group of fifteen, the guides were giving me fifteen different solutions. I had a hypnotherapist trained by the Michael Newton Institute come up and do a talk; she then conducted a group regression. Some of the students regressed, some slept and one of the men snored, but I suppose everyone got what they needed.

That night, I tried something completely different. I did an experiment called 'Faces.'

I found it in Brian Weiss's book *Many Lives, Many Masters.* It involved having a meditation and then pairing up. The idea is to sit very close to your partner and watch their face. This was in a dim light, similar to candlelight. The class sat very quietly, somewhat astonished as they watched their partners' face change again and again. There were gasps of amazement and some tears. At the end of the exercise, they had to describe what they were seeing. Then the tears really flowed as the faces of those in spirit were described with an accuracy not otherwise known. Remember that these people had never met and I had not encouraged anyone to share photos. They were all still strangers and had not started to reveal their pain privately to each other. So this small exercise really opened up everything. The healing began with a vengeance. They were healing each other.

Each morning of the retreat also found us doing Chi Gung with the retreat caretaker. He was a portly man who seemed far from fit, but looks can be deceiving.

He 'Chi Gunged' us out of the water! Chi Gung is an excellent form of energy work that can really help clear blockages in the flow of energy throughout your body. I have found grief can truly block the flow of energy in a big way. If you cannot find a suitable teacher, I suggest you buy a DVD or at least go for a gentle walk each day.

On the last day of the retreat, we practiced working with energy in the form of psychometry (holding personal items) and also aura extension. We talked about signs from heaven and looked to the universe for signs of animals, numbers, dreams and music. It was a wonderful weekend, but it had to end. Everyone was dismayed to have to leave. Two days had not been enough. The results, however, were heartening. I had set my dates for the next retreat and already had some of them coming back, but this time it would be four days.

With each day, I had learned much about what to put in the next retreat and what to take out. I had decided to include Peter Smith to do some past life and LBL regressions over the four days and I already knew the areas I wished to focus on.

I was quite happy with my first retreat and departed the mountain with lightness in my heart.

Chapter 26

Patrick was fascinated with the work I did. We had been dating for about a month when he asked me why I didn't go on television. I asked him how that would ever happen. He told me that he thought it would. I argued the point, claiming that Australian television would never go for it. He argued back. I got very huffy about it all and basically told him we would never work out because he was just too pigheaded. I also had an added worry, Rebmen, who was not taking my new situation very well. He was intensely jealous of Patrick. In fact, Rebmen was the main reason I had stayed single for nearly four years. Though I did not want to be his woman anymore, I didn't want to hurt him by going out with someone else. I had also lived in the same house for so long that it was really out of the question. I suppose I had put myself in a manipulative situation and now that I was finally free of it and living my life again, Rebmen was getting out of hand.

He threatened to take his own life. This coupled with Patrick's stubbornness made the decision to simply stop seeing Patrick much easier. I was far from happy but had no idea what to do. I called Rebmen's brothers and told them what was happening and they calmed Rebmen down again, especially when I told him I was not seeing Patrick anymore.

However, I continued to call Patrick. We could talk for hours.

Then the unbelievable happened. I received an email from a company called 'Cast of Thousands' wanting me to audition for a new psychic show starting on free to air television. I was gobsmacked and immediately called Patrick to tell him his prediction had come true only a month after he'd predicted it. I also remembered my life-between-lives regression at the end of 2007 where my guide came through and told me I was going on television so I ought to lose some weight.

The time had arrived. The message from the Kingfisher had proved correct. My life was about to change. This psychic show was to be a competition similar to the *Psychic Challenge* in the US and UK. I filled out the application form, pressed send, and as I did, I knew I would win this challenge. I knew it with my whole being.

I had no idea what to expect and was delighted to receive a call telling me I had made the first round. They wished to see me for the second round a couple of weeks later.

In my schedule, I was doing a small tour of Queensland, through Bundaberg, Rockhampton, Mackay and Maryborough. I had one spare day in the tour and ironically it was the same day as the next round of interviews for the show. I had to take a break and catch a flight back to Brisbane and be in the city by nine am. Luckily Patrick picked me up and drove me straight there. I had no idea what to expect. I was dressed in my best outfit and waited nervously for the producer, David Maher, and the president of the Australian Psychics Association, Simon Turnbull. I had known Simon for quite a few years and felt comfortable in his presence. David Maher presented as a tall, calm man with a pleasing energy about him. I liked him immediately.

My first task was to tell the producer and Simon what I did. Then they brought a woman in whom I had to read. I got a lot of hits in that first reading. She gave no feedback but I could see it in her eyes. Then I had to try to remote view an envelope. The envelope had a picture inside and I basically had to say what I thought it was. Remote viewing was something I was not used to controlling. Sure, it happened randomly in my readings, but to bring it up on demand was a new concept.

It was all over within an hour, so Patrick drove me straight back to the airport. I flew back to Rockhampton and then drove the long four hours to Mackay. I was sworn to secrecy about the project and it nearly killed me as I hate having to keep secrets. I still had little idea about the whole concept except that only seven mediums would compete and that there would be no prize money. I also knew that about three hundred had applied for the competition.

To say that I was excited is an understatement, but I kept on going. Mackay turned out to be a wonderful show, but my 'green room' was bad. I was playing at a club and the only dressing room they had was an empty men's toilet, which really did give a whole new meaning to 'green room.'

There was one reading that night I know changed a family forever and I am happy it did. The sceptics are sometimes gently guided to the spiritual core of their being most unsuspectingly and when this happens, it truly is a most wonderful occasion.

After the Mackay show was the long drive home, twelve hours all told. I went home and waited for the call from the producers to know if I had made it to the next round: the top fourteen. I was like a cat on a hot tin roof with every phone call. I wanted to do this challenge with all my heart. I had no idea what channel it would be on or what the name of the show was, only that this was it: this was my one big chance to get the people of Australia to open up to spirituality in a massive way. I knew I was going to be a part of it.

I was really sweating on it all working out. I had another small tour planned for northern New South Wales, taking in Ballina, Coffs Harbour and Taree. I was praying the next round would fall during my week off.

Finally the phone call came. I had made it to the top fourteen and I now had to go to the Fox Studios in Sydney. There, I would try out in front of cameras and all the producers of the show. Magically, it was bang on during my week off. The producers paid for my airline ticket to Sydney. I went to the airport very early on a cool morning and waited for my plane. I knew that there was another psychic travelling on the same flight. I spotted her immediately and we waited together, heads buzzing with excitement.

I had never been to a television studio before this. The Fox Studios in Sydney are housed in the old Sydney showgrounds. We were delivered by taxi and ushered to a room by the lovely assistant, Lauren. I knew that Ezio, my best friend in the field, had also made it to the top fourteen, and so he should have. I also knew two others, but the rest were strangers to me. All of the psychic arts seemed to be represented in this motley crew. Ezio and I were mediums, there were some other mediums, a Reiki Master, a medical intuitive, card readers, pagan witches and clairvoyants. I had a feeling the producers were looking for a mixture of practices and I quite liked the concept. The idea of showing a broad range of gifts to the general public of Australia was appealing.

We had a series of challenges to perform on the first day. Remote viewings, reading the producers, seeing how quickly we could get four hits, were just a few of the tasks. It was a long, drawn-out day and obviously a taste of things to come. We had to sit still for ages while the camera panned in and out on our faces. It was hard to keep a straight face at times, and it all felt very surreal. The different personalities in the room were amazing. I sat with Ezio most of the day and was so happy he was there. It was like having your family member along for one of the most important days of your life.

In fact, we were making Australian television history. Right there in Sydney, were gathered fourteen psychics flown in from all over Australia. We were taken from the offices to the studio, and truly must have looked like deers in headlights. I know I did. Everywhere we looked, we could see that this was big. There were actors around; the great Hugh Jackman was filming his hit movie *Wolverine* on that very day.

After a very long day we were sent back to the airport in taxis and told they would be in touch very soon. I hate waiting! My guides have always told me I need to observe patience. So it was time to practice what they preached. Patience!

Chapter 27

There was no time to sweat. I had to leave for the next tour of shows. I have always loved northern New South Wales. Both coastal views and mountain greenery collide to bring a pleasing mixture of colour and fresh air. I have travelled and conducted shows in this region since I began my work. The only town I avoid is Kempsey. It is much too close to the beginning of my journey so many years ago. It is where my daughter was both conceived and taken. Perhaps the pain of losing a daughter or a son doesn't quite leave us.

There was one particular daughter I have grown to love in my work, and though I had met her many times before, this beautiful Spirit child named Dani greeted me when I took to the stage at the Ballina RSL.

Dani was born in a small town hospital on January 20, 1983. Her doctor was immediately concerned and sent her to a large children's hospital. This tiny newborn girl had extensive heart problems and was not expected to live more than three days. Her parents Geoff and Wendy were distraught by the news and waited anxiously by her side until miraculously she was sent home. She wasn't quite out of the woods and her health would have to be watched carefully. For the next eighteen months, this little rebel refused to let her health beat her and she continued to thrive, amazing her doctors. Despite her good health, the doctors decided to operate to rectify some of her problems. Their good intentions nearly killed her. Not only was the operation a complete failure, but she also had to be revived straight after the operation.

Dani pulled through with all the zest and courage of a 'prizefighter,' and only a month later her younger brother was born. The family lived an idyllic life in the coastal region of northern New South Wales. They were a happy family, and both Geoff and Wendy strived to bring as much happiness as they could. At age nine, young Dani enjoyed a trip to Hawaii and only a year later, she went to Fiji. A life loving young lady, with a tomboy streak, who loved fishing and crabbing. Her only limitations were to take it easy and not get involved in sports or anything that would tax her 'funny' heart.

During her teenage years, her birth problems returned to haunt her and she spent frequent overnight trips in hospital. Dani took it all in her stride and soldiered on. No heart problem was going to stop this determined young lady. She detested anyone feeling sorry for her and always kept her sunny attitude. Her positive energy rubbed off on her family. Instead of wrapping her in cotton wool, they encouraged her to live her life to the fullest. She enjoyed time with both parents and adored her younger brother, Scott. They were best friends as well as siblings.

When she was seventeen, the specialists recommended she visit the Heart Lung Transplant team but she refused and continued to get on with her life, defying fate. Destiny has a way of moving into your life without warning.

In December 2002, at age 22, Dani suffered serious heart failure. There was no possibility to avoid the visit to the transplant unit now. It was time, and time was limited until an appropriate transplant became available. She needed a heart and also lungs because they were so deteriorated that they wouldn't keep up with a new heart. There was nothing to do now but take it easy, live life to the fullest and wait for the phone call that would change her life.

It came seventeen months later, on July 12, 2004. There was no time to wait. The organs were flown to Sydney and Dani was to meet them. A twelve-hour operation, which proved difficult and dangerous, had the doctor doubting it would work. He prepared Geoff and Wendy for the worst. A second operation performed the following day proved just as difficult. Once again, our heroine pulled out her superwoman strength and made the doctors' concerns look silly.

She pulled through and over the next two years, lived as any normal woman in her twenties in Australia: partying, playing with her friends and being a general ratbag. She had blossomed into a beautiful woman and the world just sighed when she breezed into their energy field, drawing in her strength and beauty. Like fresh air and sunshine, Dani invigorated many lives with her upbeat and optimistic attitude. She was an example of positive living and thinking.

In January 2007, Dani developed serious lung problems. She was rushed to hospital and had two long stays over the following five months. For the previous two and half years, she had been a picture of health but was now bed-ridden and breathless. After all these years, her body was giving up. No further treatment would avail. There was nothing left to do but wait for the inevitable. All the support and love she had given to her friends now came back to her tenfold. They visited, watched movies with her, and along with her family gave her all the love she deserved.

The darkest day in the lives of Dani's family and friends arrived at 11.40am on October 23, 2007. The angels wanted her home and she drew her last breath surrounded by people who adored her. As she closed her eyes, an ache began to beat in the hearts of those she loved. They had watched her defy the odds so many times. The doctors had given her only three days at the beginning of her life, but she had managed to claim twenty-five years. For her family there would never have been enough time. A soul and life as bright and uplifting as Dani's couldn't just leave, there had to be more.

Wendy went on a frantic search for answers. She devoured books on mediums and wished with all her heart that she could find one to give her the experiences she was reading about. Then she heard about me. I had conducted readings in Ballina for a family whose daughter had passed away in the Bali bombings. Wendy asked if they still had my number. When she called, it turned out to be my old office number, which had long been disconnected. Wendy was disappointed and decided it just wasn't meant to be.

Dani's spirit decided otherwise.

The clock in her room had been dislodged the Christmas following her death. It had stopped at 11.40, precisely the time Dani passed away. Wendy took this as a sign and decided to leave it on the wall stopped on the fateful time. The day Wendy tried to call me and gave up, she went to Dani's room and laid on her bed in frustration. Out of the silence, she heard a ticking. She looked up and saw that the clock had started again. She knew this was a sign from Dani not to give up looking for me. That afternoon, she found out my number and called for an appointment.

When I first met Wendy and Geoff, I immediately felt the presence of Dani. Her personality and description of herself was spot on. I could see her beautiful face swimming in my third eye vision. She took me to her home in my mind's eye and I was able to describe her room. I saw the french doors out to the veranda, and the gardens with the view from her bed. She was clear and precise. I remember actually saying a D name like Daniel, but her parents missed it. She told me about her boyfriend, and also about a plaque that had disappointed her mum. She talked about her final days. Like most people in deep grief, some of the validations I gave were missed on that first day. As usual, they were picked up later, like the plaque and even her name, which had been missed. However, Dani wanted more for her mum, so I called Wendy a couple of weeks after the first reading.

Dani talked about taking the stickers off her car. She had been very fond of car stickers and when her parents sold it, they took her stickers off and put them on the wall. She described her beloved animals and her brother came into focus. This lovely spirit gave all she could to help her family. There were many validations and memories shared, and every time I talked to her mum she told me recent gossip and more validations.

Then in May, only a month after her first reading, I had the show in Ballina. I knew some people would be there for Dani but was not prepared for the complete takeover. It seemed that at every table I went to, Dani came in to say hello to another friend and give a message. Her brother was there and she zoomed in on him as well. It was a magic show and one made even more magic by the sunshiny Dani.

Dani's story is far too familiar to many families across Australia. So many parents are forced to sit by and watch their kids struggle for breath and eventually return to the realms, taking away the light in their family's life.

There is no cure for some of the diseases in this world, no cure for a faulty heart or low-functioning lungs. I can only imagine the pain and frustration felt by the parents of these children when faced with low odds. Dani's family were told she would only live three days and they were given twenty-five years. That is twenty-five years of smiles, memories and unconditional love which still extends from the spirit world. This amazing young spirit still plays with the clock upon the wall to this day, successfully making it stop at 11.40 more often than not. This family has never stopped being thankful for the extra time they received.

If you are missing your child, remember you had a certain amount of time and that is all you were given. During his or her life, your child or loved one taught you and gave you so many moments to be cherished. My daughter passed at the age of four, but I still look back thankful she chose to lighten my life for four years. Try not to focus on what you feel 'should have been.' Do not think that their life was 'cut short.'

They were here for as long as they were and this time is where your focus should be, not on what you feel you missed out on. Take the time to reflect on what you may have learned from your loved one such as unconditional love or laughter. Dani left laughter and sunshine. My daughter left unconditional love and hope. What wonderful gift did your loved one leave you?

Chapter 28

After Ballina, we set off to do the remaining two shows of this small tour. I was bursting inside, as this was the week I would hear if I had made it to the top seven for the psychic television show. I truly thought I had because I knew in my heart that I would win it, but you know, I am human, and I still wanted the actual word from the studios. It was a frustrating drive, as quite often we would lose mobile phone reception. We finished the show at Coffs Harbour, and I still hadn't heard from the producers. I was now starting to doubt myself. Maybe my ego was driving me here and not my true psychic ability? Or perhaps, I just wanted to do something like this so bad that I had imagined all the signs. I was still seeing signs. As some of you know, I see signs in numbers and at that time, I was seeing a new number pattern: 7- 3 -1, in that order, and also 3- 3 -1. My guides have always communicated with me via some type of number system, so these new ones became my television show numbers.

We headed to Taree and settled in. I was on radio the following morning at Max FM and 2RE with my mate, Craig. I was now at a complete bursting stage. I wanted so much to hear I was on the show. I told Craig about it and he was as keen as mustard I should go on. He had supported me and believed in my gift for a few years now, as did quite a few other regional radio jocks around the country.

I was in between calls from listeners when I received a message. It was Kirsty from the Cast of Thousands. I think I nearly fainted when she told me I was in the top seven and that filming would start very soon. I had some paperwork to do and then they were flying me down to Sydney for the next six weeks!

Craig, Debbie and I jumped around the studio like maniacs and then I had to calm down to do the next reading. I was on the precipice of a new life and my mind was trying to pull it all together. My guides and instincts were correct. I was so happy to be chosen, very flattered and could not wait to get started.

The Taree show was the next night, and I will never forget a very forward and honest spirit. I clearly remember this spirit; She had a blue dress on. I was talking to her daughter when in my third eye vision, I saw the spirit go over to my chair on the stage, sit down, lift her leg and pass wind noisily. I nearly choked with surprise. When I relayed with full action movements what I had seen to the audience member, she very calmly said, "Now I know it is her. That is definitely my mum." Naturally, the rest of the audience roared with laughter.

It never ceases to amaze me what spirits show me.

The following day, we set off back home to Brisbane. I was buzzing, not just from a very successful and healing tour, but also from the news of my upcoming experience.

It was not long before things got underway. It was all to be filmed and on television by the 5th of August 2008 and it was now mid-May. There were to be five episodes in total and filming was to start immediately. We were flown to Sydney again to meet each other and to film our personal sequence where we talked about our individual gifts. All told there were: two mediums, Ezio De Angelis and I; a medical intuitive, Amanda Rousetty; a Reiki master, Jason Betts; two clairvoyants, Rayleen Kable and Mitchell Coombes; and a witch, She` D`Montford.

It was a lot of fun on that first day. The make-up lady had to determine our colouring to make us look as best we could on screen. We also had a wardrobe man who had to work out what our look was going to be. So we were preened and pruned. Photos were taken, clothes were discussed, and images were created. The wardrobe man dubbed me 'Rock Chick.' I was happy with that as it meant I could be myself. Ezio was dubbed 'Corporate Guy!'

They finally revealed the name of the show: 'The One.'

The next day, we were taken to different locations around Sydney to be filmed for the opening scenes of the show. I thought it would take just a little while, but I was wrong. I was taken to Bondi golf course and filmed on the cliffs with the water and blue sky in the background. Basically I had to stand, smile and try not to squint. Sounds easy? Wrong! When producers have a particular idea in their mind, they pull out all stops to achieve it. So there I was on a cliff at Bondi golf course, with a camera rolling backward and forward in front of me, trying to smile nicely with reflectors faced in a way to catch the light. Unfortunately, the light from the reflectors smashes you straight in the eyes. They tell you not to squint and to hold that smile. You smile, your jaw begins to ache and then the strangest thing happens. Well, it did to me.

Out of nowhere, a dog came running through all of the cabling and cameras, and then the sprinklers started. What a mess! The camera guys were running everywhere, the dog tearing off, water spraying over everything and a man running after the dog. The producer was not happy. It had been arranged for the sprinklers not to be on. The caretaker claimed they were turned off as arranged and thought that perhaps the golf course ghost had started this drama. The make-up lady and I laughed so much that my stomach hurt. I was not sure about a ghost, but it sure stopped my jaw aching for a while.

All up, we spent almost five hours shooting a one-minute segment, which I found incredible at the time. By the end of the six weeks, I realised it was just the way it was. It was all about art as one producer liked to say: art, art, art!

Andrew Daddo was the host and I must admit to being a little star-struck when I first met him. He was the first real celebrity I had ever met. He is a very down-to-earth man and I really did like him immediately. He joked around a fair bit and I appreciated his sense of humour. We had yet to meet the judges, sceptic Richard Saunders and witch Stacey Demarco.

The very first thing we were asked to do was to predict who would be in the top three and most importantly who would win. As soon as I asked, my guides gave me three names: myself first, Ezio De Angelis and then Amanda Rousetty. We were filmed in a dark room with candlelight, a writing desk and an old-fashioned pen and ink. It sounds easy to walk over to a table, sit down and write the names you have chosen, right? Well, maybe not for me. I am not known for my elegance or grace, and it took about three takes for me to get it right. To make matters worse, I ended up getting ink all over the pen and myself. Mitchell Coombes who was directly after me was not so happy with the ink on the pen. It took quite a bit to get it off!

The first challenge we had was to find a lost boy in the bush. I had been trying to practice this skill with Patrick and Jack in Brisbane before I left, and was really getting quite good at it.

On the day of the challenge, we all had a turn and once we did, we were separated from the others. It was quite perplexing, as the young boy pretending to be lost was an actor and didn't really show a lot of emotion.

We were given maps, a picture of him, and an object to hold. The idea was to use psychometric skills and remote viewing. I also tried to use a pendulum. These skills are not normally used in my day-to-day work, so in a way it was like learning new skills on national television. I did my best but also 'did' my knee.

While I was trying to find the boy, I went down into a hole and my knee twisted painfully. It swelled up immediately, but I was on a time limit of fifteen minutes so I had to keep going. I did find the boy. I could see him, but my knee was holding me back and I didn't quite make it on time. Close enough, I was happy with the result. During the search for the boy, three of us were drawn to the same area. In that area, we all felt quite sick and when we discussed it later on, we felt that maybe something more sinister had happened there. We never did find out though. I wish we had.

The studio work was where I felt I shone the most. I will never forget doing the psychometric challenge. There were one hundred and fifty people in the studio audience. Twenty-one members placed a personal item on a tray. Our job was to use the object in order to find its owner. I chose a beautiful ruby ring for no reason except that I quite liked the look of it.

As soon as I picked it up, my body and head went on autopilot, and I found myself looking over to one section of the room. I was up first, so I walked straight to that position. The next part of the task was to read the object and tell as much information about the owner as possible. I found myself looking directly at a woman in red and a lot of information started to pour out, like names and illnesses. I was doing a full medium reading. I was almost out of my five-minute timeframe when my guides said, "Look up, the ring belongs to the lady in black!" I looked up and immediately connected my energy to the woman in question. I mentioned three things and my time was up.

When I was asked whom the ring belonged to, I admitted to reading the wrong woman, but felt it belonged to the lady in black. Spot on! Both women were interviewed and, as it turned out, I was correct with both readings. I was thrilled with the result and happily anticipated the next challenges.

The container challenge was a tricky one. The idea was to find contraband in one of the hundreds of containers of a shipping yard in Sydney. Simon Turnbull had been brought in as one of the consultants on the show. His speciality was remote viewing, so once again this was a remote viewing challenge. We had been having practice sessions with him. What we had to do for practice was to try to describe a photograph hidden in an envelope. This is not easy. The best way to work with this form of remote viewing is to record whatever impressions you get. For example, water may come into your mind as blue, or you may find yourself drawing wavy lines, but the thing is to not 'second guess' yourself and to simply write or draw what comes in immediately. In most instances this will be correct.

I ended up having some success in the practice sessions, but nothing I was pleased with. When we were taken to the shipping yard, we had to apply these new skills to finding hidden contraband in the containers. When I closed my eyes to meditate, I decided to focus on a forward meditation. What I did was I placed my mind forward to the time when the container was opened. I looked for the colour, the direction it was facing and anything else that might be useful, including letters or numbers printed on the container.

In my third eye vision, I saw a brown container. I took note of the direction it was facing, and then saw the letters and numbers: CBU and 171. I also noticed that if I had my back to the container, I would see a yellow crane. With all these things in mind, I set off.

Once again, we had a fifteen-minute time frame to complete the challenge. My heart was beating fast and I looked for the crane first. I then found a brown container facing the correct direction. When I looked on its door, I saw the same letters and numbers. I was only 9 minutes in and although a little voice in my head was claiming otherwise, I second guessed myself and dived straight in. My choice would be this container.

Well, it was the wrong one. When I thought back on my vision, I clearly remembered the crane being in full vision. When the correct container was revealed, it turned out I had all the numbers, colour and letters correct, and there was the crane in full vision. I was so frustrated! So close, but so far. I was only about fifty feet from the right one.

The Olympian challenge was a lot of fun for me. We were handed a bag with the medal belonging to our Olympian. I have never watched the Olympic games. So for me, it was like a double blind exercise. I was handed a satin bag and was able to touch but not look at the medal. I felt like it was a silver medal and also that this Olympian would not be competing in the 2008 games. I kept seeing an arrow and felt a male energy. After five minutes, my

Olympian entered the stage and ended up being swimmer Geoff Hugel. I am embarrassed to admit that at the time, I really did not know who was walking up the stage or what sport he competed in. He, however, was impressed. I read him psychically for a further five minutes and kept seeing a car and also something to do with his family and brother in particular. I saw he had tossed up between swimming and football as his chosen sport. The whole time, Geoff stood smiling and his warm personality shone all over me. I truly felt this guy could be a very nice man. He confirmed most of what I had said, and later on told Andrew Daddo that if I had hit him any harder, he would have been knocked off the stage. I was more than happy with the results.

The whole time I was in Sydney, the producers rented an apartment for me not far from the studios. I loved it. It was a long way from home, but I made it my home. Some of the other participants were flying back and forth, but I felt that if I stayed, my head would be in the right mind frame and I would have a clearer channel. If I kept flying home on weekends, I would not be able to settle, and worse than that, there was a chance they would change rooms around. I really did not want to interrupt my flow. The apartments were very nice, nicer than my own home at the time. So I became quite adept at travelling without a car and totally enjoyed living in the city.

There was to be a major challenge each week as well as a studio challenge. On week two, it would be time to say goodbye to two challengers. The first four psychics to be evicted would be the judges' choice. Then the Australian public would vote who out of the top three would be 'The One.'

The first two to go were both clairvoyants, Mitchell and Rayleen. I know they were disappointed, but this was a competition and the rules had been set.

The remaining five contestants were sent to Melbourne for the next part of our challenge. We were off to see if we could find Ned Kelly's bones. Our first part of the task was going to the Melbourne museum and seeing if we could pick up anything psychometrically from the armour Ned wore in his final shootout. Unfortunately, we were only able to do this through the glass. I was not confident that it would work. From that point on however, I started to hear a voice with a soft Irish brogue talking to me. It is hard to tell at times when doing psychic work, especially in challenges like this, how much is real and how much is imagined. To say I was sceptical is an understatement. I felt I could not distinguish between my own views and my psychic impressions. The challenge was on though, so I had to shake off my scepticism and have faith that I was receiving psychic impressions. The next part of this challenge involved going to the Old Melbourne gaol at night to the place where Ned Kelly was hung. This I found very difficult. My logical mind refused to believe any spirit would hang about a cold old gaol. In all my work as a medium, I have been given the impression that spirits hover where they feel the most love, whether it is on Earth with people still living, or in the spirit realms surrounded by universal love, or even alternating between the two. I have not seen a reason for a spirit to remain in a graveyard or at the scene of their death. It just doesn't make sense.

I walked into that gaol in doubt, one part of me wondering how I was going to get through this challenge, and the other hearing the same Irish brogue I had the day before. Doubt started to prick my sceptic barrier. Could there be 'ghosts' in this gaol? Some of you may be reading this, shaking your head and wondering how a medium could not believe in ghosts. Ghosts refer to entities that are stuck in a place because they wish to stay in the place of death. However, spirits are the soul essence left behind after physical death. Because I can see no reason to stay in a place of death, the concept of 'ghosts' and haunting evades me. It just doesn't make sense to my spiritually driven mind.

Through this whole book, I have strived to tell you what happens to spirit after physical death, and here I am, telling you about my challenge to find Ned Kelly's ghost and bones.

I would be a liar if I told you I felt nothing that night, because I did. I felt a spirit walking beside me speaking with a soft Irish brogue. I felt a spirit hand squeeze my right buttock. I told that spirit telepathically that he was a cheeky so-and-so, but he had a nice firm hand. I made a friend of that spirit. I am sure of it. I felt him laugh. I walked up the hallway to the top of the stairs with my new friend in tow. All the while, I could hear his accent, soft and comforting. He showed me his beautiful gold pocket watch and dangled it enticingly before my eyes. I walked straight to the gallows and felt my throat constrict, my breath escaping my body. I knew this was caused by the fear imprinted in the walls of this death area. In fact, it is quite common for death to stain an area with the energy of fear, which can be felt by sensitive people. It does not, however, mean there is a ghost there replaying the horror in his mind.

I was in awe of this Irish spirit. It is my theory that mediums have a special light visible to spirits. This could explain why they flock around us so happily.

Chapter 29

The next day, we had to go to Pentridge Jail and try to locate the place where a few months earlier, a mass grave had been found. It was believed Ned Kelly's bones were amongst the find. His bones had gone missing eighty years earlier when the Old Melbourne gaol had been closed, and some of them had been exhumed and re-interred at Pentridge.

Once again, remote viewing techniques were to be used. We were kept well away from the site in a room with no view of the searching area. There was major building work happening at the time and there was mud, lots and lots of mud. I sat in the room and this time used a pendulum to locate the area, and then meditated in hope of remote viewing the area. This time in my meditation, I saw loose red bricks, a ute, a 44 Gallon drum and a dilapidated building. When it was my turn, I was given some gumboots and off I went. As soon as I set off with my fifteen-minute timer on, I heard my Irish man whisper in my ear. "Go straight to the back," he said. So I marched on without stopping. I came to the end of a building and walked around the back of it. There was more mud than I had imagined. I was standing right next to the dilapidated building. It looked exactly as I had seen it in my meditation. I kept walking and then I saw the ute. This had to mean I was close, so I looked for loose red bricks. There were heaps of them in the mud pit. I had to go down. I clomped down and with each step my boots became heavier and heavier. In fact, it looked like I had big mud balls on the end of my legs! Time was ticking and I needed to find my drum. I went over to the loose red bricks and looked to my left whilst facing both the ute and the old building. The Irish voice was urging me to think carefully. On my left, there was not one but two drums about fifty meters apart. I lined myself up with the back drum and used the building, red bricks and ute as a reference point. I listened frantically for my Irish man to tell me if I was right. It looked okay to me. It felt okay as well. Time was up, so I had to make a choice. I chose to stay right where I was.

As it turned out, I was the closest to the point and therefore the winner. In fact, had I walked up to the first drum and stayed in the same line, I would have been dead on target. I was pleased and gave myself a pat on the back. Finally, I had won a major challenge and all with the help of a softly spoken Irish spirit. I like to think it was Ned Kelly helping me out. Goodness knows why he would. Perhaps was he enjoying the challenge as much as we were. I found out later that the gold watch was a very significant object. It seems old Ned had stolen a gold watch from one of the guards and liked to tease the other prisoners with it by waving it enticingly before their eyes…

The studio challenge that week was a rock-and-roll challenge. We were to stand on stage in front of a hidden item, which had belonged to a deceased rock star. Each of us had five minutes, blindfolded, to handle the item whilst attempting to glean clues, using psychometry as our tool for psychic identification.

I was last in this challenge. Waiting anxiously, I was quite fascinated by the impressions my fellow psychics were receiving. As each psychic was having their turn, an image of the deceased rock star was displayed on a large ball above our heads. Ezio had Michael Hutchinson's jacket; She` had the great Freddy Mercury's wrist band; Jason had Billy Thorpe's guitar; Amanda was lucky enough to have John Lennon's music award; and I was handed a pair of satin pants belonging to the magnificent Bon Scott of AC/DC. I had all the clues but was unable to get the right name. When I realised I had Bon's pants in my hand, being a long time fan of the great Bon Scott, I actually cried a little on stage. I didn't want to give them back. How cruel of the producers not to give these items to us as gifts for a job well done!

That week the judges voted off She` D`Montford. The remainder of us had no rest. We went straight into the coming week challenges. We had to do medical intuitive work, try to identify a celebrity behind a screen, and do an airport challenge. The medical intuitive test was a lot of fun. The producers took us to the streets to approach random strangers. We asked them if we could psychically sense what illnesses they had suffered. We had a great response and I could not believe how easy it was. Basically, what I did was clear my mind and attach my energy to the person in front of me. In my mind, I knew that whatever pain I felt once tuned in would belong to the person. I truly had no idea how good I was at this. All these years of accessing spirits and how they had died made performing this task on the living very easy for me. When doing this, it is important to have faith and trust, and for once, I approached this task with everything I had. We also had to perform this on stage. Once again, I was blown away by how easy it was for me. I do believe my 'patients' were impressed as well.

The airport challenge was my least favourite of all the challenges. In my opinion, it was not set out properly to give a nice clear channel to each person. We had to match a bag with its owner. Originally, we were to do this on an aircraft with each person in individual seats, but this was not deemed possible, and the travellers had to stand outside the plane instead. To make the shot 'camera friendly,' they had to bunch all the travellers together. This caused the energies to mix together and it was impossible to tell who was who. I picked all around my guy, and none of the others had any success either. Of all the challenges, this was perhaps the least fair on psychics, but the sceptics were delighted.

The final challenge of week four was the celebrity challenge. My celebrity was Guy Leech, Ironman champion. I was able to get quite a few things right, and as we walked off stage, Guy admitted to me that he had been sceptical, but because of my accuracy was now prepared to be a bit more open-minded. Throughout this television show, my stage work in my own field had been satisfying but not my best. It was harder than in my normal shows where I know what time I will be starting and finishing. With television, you can never rely on a certain start time. You may be told a certain time, but there can be many delays if something breaks - like a light - or if scenes need to be re-shot.

Behind the scenes, we all had various techniques to get into the zone. I like to be completely by myself before a show, so I had asked for a green room for my own personal use.

It is essential for me to have half an hour before any psychic work show, during which I meditate and raise my vibrations to the highest possible point. More times than not, I would do this only to be told there would be a delay. I would have to come back down, as the vibration needed for medium work is very hard to hold for too long. In truth, it should be taken up and held for no longer than three hours. I have found this out by trial and error.

This has always been the way I work best. The days on location and in studio were very long days, so you can imagine that going up and down all day was very draining. I did not feel I was working at my optimum.

Chapter 30

Jason Betts was the next to be voted off. We were now down to the final three.

Ezio, Amanda and I were the final three, just as I had predicted. I was the only one to have correctly predicted the outcome. In time, we would see if I also had the order right.

In my heart, I knew I did.

Week five was the last week. The judges had now finished their work and it was up to the Australian public to vote. We had only two more challenges left: a trip to the centre of Australia to try to locate the body of backpacker Peter Falconio, and one more stage presentation of our own modality.

There was a moral and ethical challenge for me to deal with as it is not in my nature or calling to find missing persons. This type of work can open up already aching wounds for the parents or family of the missing or deceased, causing them much pain. I have always wanted to heal grief, not to stir it. The Falconio challenge put me in a position where, for the first time in this program, I would have to work against my own ethics.

There is not a single person in Australia who doesn't have a thought or opinion about this tragedy. I am no different. I felt that I knew too much and that I already had a strong opinion on what had happened. Peter Falconio went missing in the centre of Australia, near the very small town of Barrow Creek, in July 2001. Although Peter's body was never found, the police were led to a man named Bradley Murdoch who was consequently arrested.

As a medium, it is best to work with no information at all. The three of us were handed a condensed booklet of a novel. We were told to read it so that we had background information. This had me unsettled. I thought we had been given too much, and on top of that, I would have preferred to speak directly to Peter's parents. In my heart I know that Mr and Mrs Falconio wait every day for their son to come home and will do so until either his body is found or they pass away. I really wanted their permission, but the producers were not successful in getting us any closer to the parents. Each day leading to the trip, I prayed for some answers on how to deal with this challenge. Eventually, I realised that there might be a chance for us to find something. Perhaps we might very well be the answer to the Falconios' prayers. In my heart, I knew that if we were unsuccessful, good karma would balance this out.

I had never been to Alice Springs or to the centre of Australia, and I was looking forward to that part of the challenge. In addition, we would be flying in a helicopter! Although slightly apprehensive, I was a little excited about that as well.

The centre of Australia has to be seen to be believed. There is a connection there amongst the red dirt and flat ground that is both surreal and spiritual all at the same time. It is like a magnet that reaches into your soul and draws you closer to the Earth despite yourself. It is magical and mystical, and your soul memory is awakened to all things ancient. Time is slowed yet hastened, and I can understand why some never return to the cities after feeling the powerful pull of this sacred soil.

I was under a powerful spell the minute I stepped on the ground. A part of me is now longing to go back to feel the magic once again. I am a small part Aboriginal myself and I immediately felt the dreamtime surround me, even though this culture is really quite foreign to me. We were driven straight from the airport at Alice Springs to a small roadhouse not far from Barrow Creek. This would be our accommodation for the next two nights. The rooms were tiny but comfortable. Amanda and I were sharing. We had to have make-up put on immediately, as filming was to start that afternoon. It was rushed. Not as much time to breathe in the soil as I had hoped. We were driven to the site of the murder and taken right to the spot where Peter had been killed. I was not sure what would happen. More often than not, my experiences on 'The One' had surprised me. Although I had misgivings that we would feel anything, I remained open-minded. I was not prepared for what I saw though. No one would have been able to convince me that I would see the actual image of Peter's death. Unfortunately, I did. The imprint of the fear he felt was forever etched in this place, almost carved into the very soil his blood had seeped into. It was like watching a movie and to this day, over a year later, I can still see that movie. I do not for a minute believe that Peter is stuck there. I know his spirit is free.

To clarify a point, it is my feelings that if a person dies in a violent manner, and if a sensitive or psychic is made aware that this is the place of death, then he or she can then heighten their vibration to a point of receiving some very accurate images of the event in their own psychic vision. I am however unsure whether we are able to pick up images if we are not aware of the murder site. I am keen to try it out though. Perhaps one day in the future, I will get this chance. I think a good test for this would be to take a psychic to a place of a little-known murder without the psychic being aware that this place holds a deadly secret, and then see if they can feel anything. This would be a great test.

The two days flew by in a flash, and all three of us were quite adamant on one particular location. We were hypnotised on the first night. In my trance, I could clearly see certain things that appeared relevant to the resting place of Peter Falconio. There was a dam called Lily Dam that was relatively new. The following day, we were taken by helicopter individually and all three of us were drawn to the dam, but Ezio was the only one who followed his heart and asked to be let down in that spot. I have to say I was disappointed that I didn't ask to be put down there as well. The dam fit the visions and it also made a lot of sense. At the time of Peter's disappearance, it may well have been in the process of being built and he could easily have been hidden there undetected.

We may never know if we were right because the police did not take anything we said or did seriously, despite the fact that all our findings were given to them. I feel they simply shrugged it off as just another loopy psychic episode. I found out later that many psychics before us had tried and failed to find Peter. All of them had approached the police. It must be frustrating and annoying for the police to have to constantly follow dead-end leads. Here we were seven years later giving them yet more psychic impressions. I am not surprised they did not follow up, although I truly wish they had.

Chapter 31

The next day, we flew back to Sydney and waited anxiously for the final challenge. This was the last time we would be filmed, and then the winner of 'The One' would be revealed. We were to perform our modality one last time and the Australian public would vote. The following week was complete mayhem with a mad rush of radio and newspaper interviews. Both Ezio and Amanda are from New South Wales and I am a Queenslander, so it became a type of 'State of Origin' for psychics. We had to get as many votes as we possibly could. We were able to invite family members and friends to the final show. Patrick was working away at the time so I invited Rebmen and Jack to be my guests. My assistant Debbie and her husband Trevor also came as support.

One of the ongoing dramas behind the scenes was in the wardrobe department. We all had our own idea of what we thought we looked good in, but these thoughts were rarely if ever matched by our wardrobe man. His facial expressions made me laugh out loud more often than not. I swear he could turn you to stone if he truly wanted to. He wanted me in dresses and heels. I hate heels. I cannot walk in them and my knees do not take too kindly to being in any type of heel for too long. Each week, a new set of shoes or boots would arrive and he would look hopefully toward the heels. I would dig my heels in and stubbornly refuse. His heartbreak was obvious. He could not consider dressing up a woman without heels. I started to feel sorry for him and promised that if I made it to the top three, I would wear the heels of his choice for the last show. He was delighted when I did, and happily showed me a beautiful set of 4" heeled boots and a dress for my final outfit. I think my knees actually groaned out loud.

The final show arrived and excitement was filtering through the green room. All the previous contestants were there as well as our families and friends. Everyone settled to watch us do our final psychic presentation. It was the first time we actually could watch each other perform a reading, so it made it even more nailbiting.

The moment had arrived and the three of us were together on stage. My heels were killing me and I was struggling to stop myself from ripping them off. Andrew Daddo asked each of us who we thought would win. I honestly replied that I had always thought I would win. Afterwards, I felt I sounded a little ego-driven but it was the truth. Ezio and Amanda both claimed they thought it would be me.

It was a very surreal and humbling feeling when I was announced the winner and handed my trophy. Everyone rushed on the stage and madness seemed to envelop me for a few moments. There were cameras flashing, people hugging and everyone was talking at once. Later, when I found my phone, I had about thirty missed calls all made at the winning moment. It was one of my proudest moments. To think that a girl who had come from so far down had just been voted Australia's Most Gifted Psychic was incredible. I knew my family in spirit were watching and knew they had somehow made this happen, but then perhaps I deserved it. Either way, on the 5th of August 2008, I was the one who won 'The One' and I will always hold that moment high in my heart.

The media madness continued in frenzy afterwards. People called the office desperate for a reading with the One. I received thousands of emails and people booked readings to the point of me having to close the books. There were so many people looking for so much. It was complete insanity. I had everyone from people wishing for a medium reading to those looking for missing cats and dogs. Ridiculous really! I wish to state right here that I do not find lost animals ever, not even my own. It is not my psychic gift. There were really heartbreaking stories from people who had family members who had simply gone missing. To be honest, I do not have that gift either. I truly only do medium work, so please clarify what type of psychic you want before begging someone to help you. I felt like I was being torn into a thousand pieces, and I had to get away.

Patrick had just returned home and squirreled me away to the Sunshine Coast to escape the media and people. It didn't matter where I went though, I was recognised everywhere. In shops, streets, service stations, you name it, I was noticed. I never really thought I had such a recognisable face until then. It was a crazy time and very hard to handle. I had people who wanted to manage me, and people who wanted to do shows. I was the latest craze for a short while and in all honesty, I am quite happy it has now died down. I am not sure how famous people handle this total invasion of privacy but I found my five minutes of fame quite distressing. There were so many upsides though. I had totally buried myself in debt since the beginning of my career as a medium, but now the shows were attracting a much larger audience and my debts were being paid. To really top it off, I was now able to find the people who really needed my help and the bereaved parents were beginning to recognise me as someone who understood.

The shows were providing me with financial stability, so I began to counsel bereaved parents for free. There were more people than just me benefitting from my success. It felt wonderful to be able to spread my good fortune. I still do. One of the major benefits of 'The One' was that it opened the eyes of the Australian public to the possibilities of psychic work in the community. The producers strived to show how psychics could be trained in remote viewing to assist search and rescue teams to find lost people in bushland, maybe even to find hidden contraband in shipping containers. It was proved that with the right training, we might even be able to identify and locate medical conditions in people. I feel the producers did their job successfully and will always admire their persistence and patience in getting this often taboo subject onto mainstream television.

There is no doubt in my mind that these two brave producers have done the spirit world and psychic community a huge favour. They have taken more people off the fence and given them something to believe in again. I am totally aware that I may not be Australia's most gifted psychic, but we had to start somewhere and I am glad I was chosen. Maybe in the future similar shows will be produced in Australia, and considering the overwhelming response, they would fare well.

Chapter 32

The following two months, life continued at breakneck speed. Patrick and I were always in each other's company, and continued to get closer. His work in New Guinea was now over and he was working in the Brisbane office. The shows continued to get bigger with more people wanting to see what the fuss was about. With each show more hearts were healed. Some readings were so intense that you could hear a pin drop in a room of five hundred people. My life was definitely a lot different than it was a year before. My work was in high demand, the bills were getting paid, and I was falling in love. I went on a small trip to regional Victoria and New South Wales in September and while I was gone, Patrick ended up in hospital with chronic breathing problems. He was a smoker and a drinker and owned two beautiful Harleys. It looked like his fast living life was catching up with him. If he continued to smoke, he would be a very sorry boy. Emphysema had gained control of his lungs, so it was time for him to make choices. He gave up the cigarettes without a backward glance and I am happy he did, as I had no intention to spend my time visiting anyone in hospital. That's what I told him anyway!

Life is so unpredictable. We need to be kind to our bodies and our spirits. With Patrick, I was having a hard time staying true to my abstinence from alcohol. I had been relatively sober for quite a few years, but with Patrick came temptation. I soon found it was okay to have fun sometimes, just not all the time like in the dark days. I was learning balance and was really enjoying my time with him. It seemed that everything in moderation was the key to balance. When I came home from my trip and he was well again, we decided it might be time to start living together. Between us we were shelling out a lot in rent and were spending time at only one place, so it made sense to give it a go. I wanted to live closer to my sons, so we focussed on their area.

Patrick understood my need to be closer. It would enable my youngest son to get a job on the weekends, and I would see a lot more of my oldest son as well. We set out to find a place to rent, but when we began to look we realised it would be better to buy. Patrick had a certain amount of capital and I had just completed six or seven very successful shows, so we were in a prime position to approach the bank. When we did, we found we were eligible for a good loan. I was scared to death. There was a lot riding on this decision, not just in terms of money but how it would affect others in my life. I knew the boys would be good with it and my business worked anywhere really, as these days most of my readings were by telephone. The biggest hesitation I had was with regard to hurting Rebmen's feelings. Some of you may be thinking I was crazy to think that way, but he was so fragile and had been looking so sad lately. He had come to a few shows and had met Patrick. I have to say he was a gentleman to the limit. I knew it hurt him greatly that I had moved on, but he was making out that he was okay. Moving in with Patrick would make it very clear to Rebmen that I was serious. Buying a house with him would spell out just how serious I was. I bit the bullet and went with my heart. Before I knew it, we had bought the most beautiful house only ten minutes away from my sons. I was over the moon. The bank now owned us but we had a new lifestyle. We had a pool and even my dogs were happy in this new house. Rebmen had finally given up his rights to George the bulldog, and I had never seen George as happy as he was when we moved in.

I kept pinching myself. I was living with a most interesting and loving man who was proud to have me on the back of his Harley, a man who loved me enough to invest money in a house with me. He encouraged me with my music and just wanted to be with me.

The shows were going magnificently and I was in love with life. It looked like my time in the sun had arrived.

Only a few days after moving in, I was doing a show in my new area. It had sold out and I nearly fried on stage. The agent who was booking my shows had asked for lights to be put straight on me. If you have ever stood under stage lights, you will know how damn hot they get. I started the show and immediately felt sweat running down my forehead. To make matters worse, I had mascara on that night and I felt like it was leaking!

I was in my old hometown, so many of the spectators had gone to school with me. I could not believe it when one woman started to ask me if I remembered her. I finally did remember two months later, and yes, that is how long it bugged me.

The club manager had decided to put fifty more patrons in the room, and I had people sitting about 6 inches from my knees! So there I was, getting 'well done' under the lights, feeling claustrophobic, with a woman I could not remember trying to get me to remember her, and trying to read someone else at the same time. It was a disaster.

That was the night I found out I could not read in the heat very well. I stopped the show and demanded the lights to be turned off. The stage was tiny anyhow, so I could not see the point of having them. The room was overflowing and these people had paid good money. Once the lights were off, I immediately started a new reading.

This woman had a husband in spirit and he was ready to go. The validations started, thick and fast, and the very last thing he told me was that she had his ring with her. When I relayed the message, she opened her hand to reveal a man's wedding ring in it. After that reading, there was no going back and the night became successful.

After each show, I spend time meeting people and signing books. While I was doing that, a woman with a heavily tattooed right arm walked up and quietly waited by the side of the table. I was drawn to her and my soul recognised something in her immediately. It was like I had to know her, or it was kinship. Whatever the feeling was, it was strong.

She handed me a card and explained that she and her partner owned a tattoo parlour, and that if I ever wanted a tattoo, she would look after me. Her name was Janine and her partner's name was Rick. I had heard of him but could not quite recall meeting him. I kept the card. Something told me to keep it, as I would be using it very soon. I had no idea why.

In the meantime, I had my first four-day retreat to conduct. Peter Smith, my hypnotist friend from Melbourne, was coming up to give the retreat participants life–between-lives and past life sessions. I was finally going to see if my theories about Newton's work would be effective in helping bereaved parents.

Chapter 33

The November retreat was over four days and we had a mix of people participating. Some had lost children and others partners.

One young couple, with the young lady very pregnant, had lost their two-year-old son, Travis, in April 2008. They arrived at the retreat in a lot of pain but with a yearning to learn how to move through their grief as a family. I found this very honourable, especially for Rick, the husband. This retreat was clearly not his 'thing', but his love for Kirsty was undeniable, and his love for his son unshakable. Kirsty especially needed to understand why such an event had happened. She felt a massive amount of guilt, quite unnecessarily in my eyes. It was now up to me to try to light the path and bring some sense into the madness and pain that had become their lives.

Kirsty and Rick had lived happily and peacefully with their two children, Travis, 2, and Tameeka, 11. Both young parents worked away from home. While Tameeka was at school, Travis was under the care of a 'daycare mum' who was living not far from their home. Travis had been with this daycare mum for a while, so on that fateful April morning, Kirsty dropped her precious cargo off and went to work never suspecting what lay ahead. Unbeknownst to Kirsty, her daycare mum and another mum had planned to take all the kids to a local park for an outing. No one was told and no one was asked. No permission slips were filled out and the two daycare mums went off with their brood of children all under the age of five. Naturally, the kids were delighted at the treat. They all ran off to play on the swings and playground equipment as the two carers sat chatting with a semi-watchful eye on all of them, except Travis.

Travis had made his way to an unsecured pond. He toddled into the water, but no one heard the splash as he was too far away. No one saw his futile attempts to save himself as his head went below the surface. No one saw Travis drown, because no one was watching. By the time someone did notice, Travis had already passed away.

In five minutes, a family's life was changed forever.

I spent a great deal of time on the subject of forgiveness, as I do at every retreat. I made both Kirsty and Rick understand that this woman would be feeling a massive amount of guilt. There was no way she set out to commit such a neglectful act, no one in their right mind would. I convinced them that if they were able to truly forgive her in their hearts, then perhaps it would make it easier for them to move through their grief.

They left the retreat with a newfound determination to pursue my ideas, but it was not long before they were knocked back to square one again. There were court battles ahead, and Kirsty and Rick were bracing up for the upcoming dramas, which would undoubtedly unfold. They were well and ready to forgive, but they first needed to hear just one word: sorry.

As each day ended, it was still not said.

I am well aware that the carer in question must have felt mountains of guilt and pain, but I also know she would have been warned by her lawyer to not say a word, just in case it was taken as an admittance of guilt. I have spent many hours on the phone since the retreat trying to calm Kirsty down, but I really do sympathise with her. I know too well how much it hurts not to hear that essential 'sorry.' I know how far that word can reach into your heart and start to heal the pain, because with it comes forgiveness.

Forgiveness after an accidental death is one of the most healing emotions on the road of grief.

It was not the first time I came across this situation.

In one case, I conducted a reading where a woman was hoping to get in contact with the young man who had died in a car accident as a result of her carelessness on the road. The spirit came through very happily and even apologised to the woman for his family. This lady had carried the guilt around for almost two decades when she had the chance to see me. She told me she had approached the parents and family of the young man to try to apologise, but their anger had been too great. She had spent all of those years tearing herself up with guilt and regret for her actions. When the reading was finished, her cheeks were wet with tears of relief. It was an honour to be able to relieve her of such a heavy burden. This was a case where I wished the family had accepted her apologies.

Then there was the reading for another young lady who unsuspectingly became involved in a suicide mission. She was driving home from work when she hit a man who was sitting in the middle of the road, drunk and suicidal. He died on impact and the poor girl was beside herself with disbelief. She was aware she was not to blame, but still needed to know if the spirit was okay. He came through and apologised for his actions. After the reading, she told me how his parents had put an ad in the paper telling her how sorry they were and also how she was not to blame. Their son was sick and had involved an innocent stranger. They wanted her to know they bore no grudge. I felt this was one of the most amazing things a family could do. Imagine the compassion of these two devastated parents, to be able to put the pain of this young stranger before themselves in one of the darkest moments of their life.

Some of you reading this may have someone to forgive, or maybe someone you need forgiving from as a result of an accident involving your loved ones. Think carefully about the situation. If they have not said 'sorry', is it because of impending court battles? If it is, remind yourself that the lawyers and solicitors may have prevented the guilty party from contacting you. You may think it shouldn't matter, but also remember that not everyone is as compassionate as you are. Some would take a 'sorry' as an admission of guilt and use it against the blamed party. I am certain that solicitors and lawyers have many reasons for silencing their clients. Put yourself in the shoes of the other party. Remind yourself that they may think that 'sorry' is not enough for a life. By approaching you, they may feel you might anger or attack them.

When I question someone else's actions, I always try to see them from the other point of view. I wonder how many of you would be able to put an ad in the paper or if it is even worth thinking about? The choice of how you deal with this touchy and sensitive issue is yours, but just a little food for thought: forgiveness will set you free and compassion will make you stronger. To forgive them for a moment of stupidity will go a long way in your own healing.

Kirsty and Rick still have a long way to go. Their situation is complicated by many factors ranging from home daycare guidelines to fencing regulations around water at playgrounds. This court case is likely to go on for a long time. In my heart, I hope the woman in question will one day slip a small note saying 'sorry' to them, because I know how much it would help heal everyone involved, but until that time, I am there for the whole family. They now have a new baby boy, Joey, who is playing a very essential part in their healing. Every time I talk to Kirsty, a chatty little Travis is keen to tell me everything they have been doing. It is obvious he still walks beside them daily.

So if there is no 'sorry', try not to dwell on it and reach toward the beautiful parts of your life, as there are so many if you look for them. Strive to forgive the unforgivable, and one day, I am sure you will succeed.

Chapter 34

The retreat was successful and I felt that everyone got what they needed. It just happened to run on the same day as the Melbourne Cup. Because of my new status as 'The One,' I had been contacted to give my Cup predictions on television, so there was a slight disruption to enable that to happen. Various radio stations had also contacted me for my predictions and even Rebmen, being the horse race mad punter he was, called me from Townsville to get my tips for the cups. So the last day of the retreat was a little bit chaotic, but nonetheless we all had fun and that was the main thing.

After the retreat, Peter Smith and I headed back to my house to relax and wind down after a very full-on four days. We analysed the retreat while Patrick plied us with food and wine. We concluded that it had been a success. This was our first venture together and we were both very happy with the results.

There was no time to rest for me though. I had another show coming up. One of the radio presenters I worked with had asked me if I would like to film one of my shows and maybe make a marketing package out of it. Patrick and I thought it would be a great idea, so I also enlisted Rebmen and asked for his help to operate my camcorder, as having two cameras would provide a better quality. He agreed and we all met up before the show.

It was a Sunday afternoon and when Rebmen arrived, I was taken aback by his appearance. He had not shaved and smelt as if he had been drinking heavily. I hugged him to say hello and felt that he had lost weight. I knew he still battled with drug addiction after we split. In fact, drugs were one of the reasons I finally decided to get my own home a year before, as I suspected he was still using.

His appearance and weight had me extremely worried. His eyes looked dull. He was not happy at all, but we were mates so I didn't question him. I just trusted that he was okay. I was about to start the show and would speak to him afterwards.

The show was great. I looked around anxiously for Rebmen afterwards to thank him for his efforts and to have a go at him about his appearance, but Debbie told me that he had left. Later, I got a text message saying, 'Great Show Prick' (He always called me Prick). I was relieved to get the message, as straight after the show, there had been a massive thunderstorm. The skies had turned an angry green and hail had poured down. This storm came out of nowhere just like a hurricane and was almost surreal in its nature, like a warning. How Rebmen got home without damage amazed me.

About a week later, Patrick and I decided that he would be my permanent manager, booking shows and travelling with me, making sure lights and sound were all in perfect order. It was a big decision as it meant he would be leaving the security of a well-paid job. We were a little under-whelmed by the efforts of my agent, as he kept booking us in smaller and smaller venues with inadequate facilities. At one venue a couple of weeks earlier, we had to contend with beer bottles, golf balls and plastic chairs being thrown on the roof, not to mention the drunkards weaving through the audience.

People were paying good money to see me and this was not good enough. We decided to hire theatres where we could. When we approached the booking agent about this, he dug his heels in, so we decided to go alone. I remember dreading telling Rebmen about this, as it had been one of his dreams to be on the road with me. He had accompanied me to many shows. His reaction was, as expected, very quiet. I knew he was hurt, but in all fairness he did not have the gift of the gab required or the people skills necessary to make a good manager. I defended my decision and he agreed that I was right.

The next day, Rebmen called me in a foul mood. We had Patrick's ex-wife visiting at the time and when I told Rebmen, he said, "Well, I won't bother you then." I could not understand why he was so angry and put it down to him wanting to ask for money. I had told him in the past that I wouldn't do that because trying to get it back was nearly impossible. So he hung up on me and I just let him go. It seemed like our friendship was falling apart and it hurt, but I was not sure what to do about it. He had become secretive and reclusive again. I knew something was going on with his daughter and he had mentioned his ex-wife to me as well, but in all honesty I am not sure I took in what he was saying. I had become consumed by my new busy life.

The following Saturday, I woke up earlier than usual. I picked up my mobile phone and saw that someone had left a message during the night. It was from Rebmen and when I read the message, a cold chill swept over my body. The message read: "Prick, I am kicking this habit. Sorry I couldn't be a better friend. Love your guts."

I called out to Patrick in a panic and he decided we were going to Rebmen's place immediately. I called Rebmen and to my relief, he answered the phone. He sounded like I had just woken him up. I demanded what the message meant and he told me that some stupid bitch had sent it from his phone. I did not understand how this could happen. I asked him if he wanted me to come over and he said that he didn't. He explained that a few months before when he had threatened to commit suicide, he was going to send that message. The previous night, he had taken a girl home and apparently she had been mucking around with his phone. He told me he would ring me back in a few minutes. I was not quite settled, but all I could think was that he had a girl. He called me and told me that she was a stupid bitch, and I replied that he should give her a go. He kept saying: 'Sorry Prick', and I couldn't understand why. I said it was great that he had a girl over. He again apologised, but I brushed it aside and gushed over the fact that he finally had a new girlfriend. I was over the moon for him. He apologised a few more times and we disconnected.

I can honestly say I had not felt as happy or settled as I did the following few hours. I had sweated and worried about the effects of my relationship with Patrick from the day I had met him, but now that Rebmen had a girl, I felt everything was going to be okay.

Later that morning, we took the big white bike to the shops. On the way home, just before our turnoff, I had a strong sense of Rebmen. My psychic vision was taken over by a strange meditation I had had a few years before where two horses were ploughing a field near a mountain. One of the horses had broken free and run off, but it kept coming back to the other horse. The other horse did not want to move. When I questioned my guides about this meditation, they explained the horses were Rebmen and I. I was the free horse and Rebmen was the one who refused to move.

That day on the bike the meditation came back, but I could now see the second horse running out of the paddock. Rebmen's horse was free and both horses were running together. I interpreted it to mean that his new girl had set him free. I felt a powerful energy at that moment, but didn't think about it until a few hours later.

Chapter 35

The phone rang at about 2 pm that afternoon. I missed the call and when I looked at it, I noticed it was Rebmen's brother, Raymond. I had remained good friends with most of Rebmen's family and was especially close to his mum, as well as brothers Raymond, Cameron and their families. I also got on quite well with Rebmen's daughter, Simone.

My knees buckled and I yelled out to Patrick, 'Oh no, he's done it!' I kept yelling, "No, no, no!" I eventually got Raymond on the phone. "He finally went and did it!" Raymond cried down the phone. "He's gone!" he said, and then it sunk in, my worst fears were confirmed. He *was* talking about Rebmen. Raymond was trying to tell me that Rebmen had killed himself. I struggled to absorb this news. He had gassed himself to death in the car. Patrick looked up to see why I was crying so loud.

It was not true, it couldn't be, but I knew it was. I had just spoken to him a few hours earlier, he had a new girl; he couldn't be dead. My worst fears had been realised and the blackness of death engulfed me again. I told Raymond I would call him back later.

I am not sure what happened afterwards apart from the blackness covering my whole being. Everything began to flashback, the message, the phone call, the weird meditation on the bike. No, Rebmen couldn't do this, he wouldn't do it to his mum or daughter; he loved them too much. Reality began to bang on my bubble of disbelief, he would do it and he had done it. Rebmen was dead.

The guilt was overwhelming. My psychic ability for once had let me down, but he had lied to me to stop me from coming over. I realised he probably passed away when I had the strange meditation on the bike. I didn't know what to do or how to be. I am not sure there is a way to be when confronted with this type of news. How could I have not seen it? I had tried to tell his family. My fears and now the nightmare prediction had come true. What was the use of bloody predictions anyway? You were never given a time or moment.

It was useless if you could not prevent the death from happening. I called my sons and broke the bad news. Jack who was very close to Rebmen wanted to come over to our place. I decided that it was a good time to get drunk and I did. I make no apologies for this as alcohol numbed the thoughts screaming through my head. I cried all night and didn't sleep much. I wanted Rebmen to talk to me but the guides wouldn't allow it, or I was too drunk. I am not sure.

There was nothing but the blackness of death, arguably the worst type of death, suicide. I still think that losing Crystal was the worst, but how can you measure pain? I was sick of pain; I had felt far too much pain from death. Rebmen knew this! Didn't he think we loved him, didn't he know everyone had had too much pain? Why had he done this? I was angry, sad, guilty, horrified and broken. I felt like I had screwed up so badly. I wanted to see his mum.

The next day, I went to his mum's house and sat with the family. They asked if I would go to the dreaded John Tonge Centre (the morgue). I decided I would, as I was having trouble imagining Rebmen dead. It felt so strange to be at his mum's without him. It had always been such a happy home, but now it too was covered with blackness. No one was smiling and Rebmen's family wanted to know why I hadn't told them. It was like being punched in the gut. The realisation hit me that I was supposed to be Australia's Most Gifted Psychic, and I couldn't tell when my best friend was about to commit suicide. They had relied on me all these years, had supported me and I guess at that moment, they may have felt let down. I explained to them about the text message and the phone call. They understood, but I was still questioning myself.

The next day was terrible. I had never been to the morgue before, although my clients had told me about it. I had only ever pictured it in my head and now I was there, in the coldness of this place. To give the staff credit, they are very good at calming the situation down and they do have a way of preparing you for the worst, but then, does anything prepare you for the sight of someone you love laying on a slab behind a glass?

And there he was, his beautiful face stilled by death, dreadlocks splayed on the pillow and his body cold as ice. Nothing can erase this picture except time itself. Rebmen looked like he was sleeping and he looked peaceful. I hoped his heart was peaceful now. His peacefulness had created unrest in my soul, a disruption of my whole self and also of his entire family. His family surrounded him, but I could only sit heavily on a chair outside of the glass. The wind was gone, the fight was over, and I had nothing left at that moment.

The funeral was massive. We all wore our favourite football team's shirt. I wore a Bulldog's team shirt, as it had been Rebmen's favourite team. As I looked around, I could not believe Rebmen had not reached out to at least one of us. If not me, why not one of the hundreds of people present? We had all loved him in our own way for different reasons. I made sure I put a Spirit Whispers staff tag into his coffin, and told him he had better be working from the other side now. Everyone went back to Rebmen's mum's place for the wake, but Patrick, Jack and I decided to stop for a little while. We would have our own wake at home.

I searched my soul for answers over the following months. I had done so many readings for families whose loved ones had committed suicide, and now here I was with the shoe on the other foot. Nothing prepared me for the hell I was plunged into. Don't get me wrong, I had gone there many times, but this was different. This hell was filled with the guilt and the fear that I might have been the cause. I tortured myself relentlessly for the first six months. I blamed my happiness for Rebmen's unrest. I took it out on Patrick and hated myself for loving Patrick. I crawled along the edge of complete self-loathing and belittled myself at every opportunity. I felt I was to blame for not just my unhappiness, but also for Rebmen's and his family's. The sad truth was that all of us were torturing ourselves in the same way, and I am sure some of his family still is. It is such a stupid thing for the suicide victim to feel we are better off without them, and worse, that maybe they can teach us a lesson through their death. Who needs this type of pain? It's bad enough in the case of an accident, but absolutely horrific when you realise this was the conscious choice of a person you loved with all your heart. Nothing is solved and I am certain that the many people who commit this somewhat thoughtless act can see their mistake far too late. I bet if Rebmen could come back, he would.

In fact, I have dreamed of him since and he indicated that although he was okay, nothing he had gone through on Earth justified the pain he put us in.

Chapter 36

In my pain, I have talked long and hard with my guides about the spiritual reasons for suicide. I have done countless readings for people who have lost someone to suicide before and after Rebmen's death. Before I had the displeasure of experiencing this type of death, I had many different theories. However, I now think a little differently.

In the past and present, I have found that people who committed suicide are usually most anxious to make contact with their families through a medium, so that they can explain that the reason they are gone is not because of the partner or the family, but because of their inability to deal with the life lessons placed before them. They are not cowards, nor are they condemned to travel eternally in some form of limbo. They are essentially your family members or friends that took on a little more than they could handle in this life.

In much the same way that a student is offered lessons to complete at school, we are all offered lessons before we descend to the earthly plane as a baby. These lessons are given to us throughout our time on Earth, and much like the student who chooses unwisely at the beginning of the term, sometimes as souls preparing for a new life on Earth, we too choose lessons or situations that our souls may be too immature for. All of this takes place in accordance with our guides before we descend. Although we may be warned that we are not ready for the chosen tasks, some of us refuse to listen and take the lesson anyway. I truly feel that this is the case in most suicide situations: the soul of the suicide victim is unprepared for the planned lessons, and akin to a student dropping out of school, it decides to drop out of life.

In my heart, I understand that we all pass when it is our time, neither a minute before nor a minute after. I have wondered if perhaps some people are destined to take their own lives, if in fact it was in their contract. As souls that constantly evolve, perhaps we get to choose the way we die in order to grasp a full range of understanding of the human nature. The more lives we live, the more our understanding grows. Not for one minute do I feel that suicide is a positive action, but if you have had someone pass over in this manner, try to look above the situation and ask yourself if this may have been a decision that was completely out of your hands. Accept your loved ones' decision and try to understand that the universe may have in fact called them home. In a lot of cases with accidents, I hear stories of how the accident victim would discuss what they wanted at their funeral just the day before their death, almost as if they knew that their time was nearly over. So with that in mind, ask yourself if this could have been the case with your loved one.

The most important thing to remember if you have found yourself in this position is to be kind to yourself and everyone else who is affected. They are no more to blame than you are, whether you think they are or not. Ultimately, it was your loved ones' decision and they could have reached out at any time to anyone, but for whatever reason chose not to. Do not consume yourself with the reason why it happened, because the quicker you can accept it, the quicker you will begin to heal. If you feel you need to forgive yourself, your loved one or anyone else involved, do it and move through this horrific time. Time is what you will need, but it is possible to survive this death.

I am now nine months down this track. I have diligently followed my own advice given throughout this book and I am feeling okay. I have stopped the blame exercise, and I am back to loving myself again. I have kept in contact with Rebmen's family and have been trying to get one of my medium friends to read them as I am far too close to the situation to do this. It is important for me to keep going for the many who need my services, and although it has been a struggle, I have come through the blackness and I am now in the blue again. I thank my guides daily for making me aware of how to heal quicker.

I had to do a show only two weeks after Rebmen's death. I did not want a part of it. I walked onto the stage numb with grief and with the full realisation that these people needed the gift I had. I explained what I had just been through and told them I would do my best. To my surprise, it went exceptionally well. I could not believe how many tragic deaths were revealed during the afternoon of that show. Then it hit me. It must have been Rebmen helping me. In life, when he had travelled from show to show with me, he was always a little morbidly let down if the show didn't have what he classified as 'The Tragics.' I thought he was horrible when he said that, but that was Rebmen and the way he thought. I am sure now that he is on the other side as a *Spirit Whispers* team member, that I will be seeing a lot more of 'Rebmen's Tragics.' I suppose in a way, he is finally living his dream of travelling with me wherever I go. What's more, he is bringing forward those whose families have been hit hard.

So I struggled on, working with my grief until just before Christmas. Finally, I was able to relax and stop work. I needed it because working with other people's grief daily is hard enough, let alone working with your own at the same time. This Christmas was to be a milestone also. Well, Boxing Day anyhow. For the first time in nine years, my family was coming to spend the day with Patrick and me. My brother also named Patrick, his partner Karen, my stepfather, Jack, and my niece Kathleen. My other son, Alan, promised me to make an appearance sometime during the day.

It was a lovely warm day and we all settled down with Christmas cheer. I was trying to keep my mind off Rebmen as this was the first Christmas without him in nine years. My little bulldog George, however, was acting strangely throughout the day. He just kept sleeping and then around two pm, he threw a fit. I couldn't believe it. I called the vets but most were closed and the only ones that were opened were so far away. I had already had a few drinks, so I stopped drinking and kept a close eye on him as advised. He was in bad shape, so I followed him around the yard until he came and lay on his bed near us all. His breathing was terrible, but he seemed settled. I relaxed a little and decided we could take him to the vet first thing in the morning.

We never made it to the vet. George passed away around ten pm that night. He had a heart attack and then he was gone. He was only eight years old! Rebmen and I had worshipped this dog and had even established shared custody when I left a year earlier. I would have him for a week, and then we would swap. When I moved to the new house, Rebmen kept saying he would come and get him and now it looked as if he had. I was in shock. It was a day shy of a month since Rebmen had passed. I was sitting with tears pouring down my face, sobbing. My heart was well and truly broken now. Dogs are such lovely souls and they love you unconditionally. When they die it is horrible. To lose George so close to Rebmen was a crime.

About forty minutes later, I was watching the back yard still crying, when I noticed a strange orange glow cover the whole yard. I looked around at the others but no one else seemed to notice, so I sat quietly and absorbed what feelings were coming through. I felt Rebmen so strongly; it was like he was right there in physical form. He had come to get George, as promised. As I looked, I could see George's spirit mix with the orange glow and then melt together. I felt such peace in that moment.

Once again, I felt a spirit I loved go through the gates, this time a little bulldog assisted by our best friend Rebmen. I started to cry tears of joy for my little mate who had given so much love and pleasure. When he moved in with Patrick and me, he succeeded in winning Patrick's heart as well.

At that precise moment, the phone rang. It was 10.40 pm and I could not imagine who would ring at such a time. When

I answered, it was Raymond, Rebmen's brother, the very same brother who had sold us George all those years ago. I truly could not believe it! Rebmen must have somehow encouraged him to call. He was drunkenly singing a Christmas carol as I stared at the phone in disbelief. I told him what had just happened and it silenced the racket on the other end of the phone. He was in shock. He too had loved George. To ring at the precise moment when I felt Rebmen take George with him, was proving me that everything I had just felt was incredibly real.

Chapter 37

As you might imagine, the Christmas season of 2008 was not especially joyous for me. Considering the amazing year I had winning 'The One,' it definitely followed the general principal of life: after every high there must be a low, and after every low there must be a high. I just didn't understand why my highs were so high and my lows so low. I truly feel that my life has had enough heartache littered throughout my relatively short time on Earth. I have now experienced every type of death and quite frankly, I have had enough. But onward and upward, as they say!

New Year's Eve brought with it a new start and new friends. We managed to get invited to some neighbour's place to play music. Patrick is a skilled musician and had been disappointed when his regular New Year's gig was cancelled. We had already decided to stay home and have a quiet one with my brother when I received an invitation from a fellow I had met on My Space. I had been talking to him via the net for years and although we had never met in person seemed to get along. He contacted me to tell me some friends of his were having a party no more than a five minute walk from our house. It was a fantastic night and we realised we were living amongst some people who truly were birds of a feather, some I had known for thirty years. They all ride Harleys and play music. It was almost like spirit was showing me I had a brand new life now, and with the New Year it was time to start it. Another person at the party was the woman who had handed me the tattoo business card a few months earlier. Her partner Rick was the guitarist as well as the tattooist.

Tattoos have been used in tribes since the beginning of time. Ancient tribes used tattoos as a symbol of rites of passage, marks of status, marks of love, or they may have been symbolic of simply belonging to a particular tribe or religion. Tattoos were brought to western society by sailors and sea-merchants who travelled the oceans and visited many of these tribes. The outcasts, like slaves, convicts and prisoners were also tattooed, which I presume is where the bad boy look came from. Tattoos are becoming fashionable again for many reasons, but one of the most common reasons is to symbolise our love for those who have left the Earth.

These days, I receive more and more validations from spirit that their relatives have gotten tattoos in their honour. In a way we have gone back to our tribal ways, as more often than not, I see groups getting the same tattoo. They may be friends or family members, which indicates to me the person who passed was an essential part of their soul essence, and perhaps their soul group.

When I met Janine again at the party, we sat and talked. I really did like her. It seemed she was hoping to swap a tattoo for a reading. Rick is well-known in Brisbane for his tattoos, and here I was hoping to memorialise my love for Rebmen and all he meant to me.

As the old year drew to a close and live music rang through the streets of our neighbourhood, I started a new life, with new friends, and designed a new tattoo to remember someone special. Life started to feel nice again.

I still had a long way to go in my grief for both Rebmen and George. When I designed the tattoo, I put in Rebmen's birthday and mine, June 16th, and kept it in line with my other ones, which portray American Indians. It made me feel good to do it and I feel it helped my healing process.

Another thing that had to be done was to get a new dog. I called several kennels and two had new puppies available in six weeks. I applied for both and that night, I had a dream where Rebmen came and told me to go with one kennel only. I thought this was a sign and pushed to get a bulldog from Rebmen's chosen kennel. I could not believe my luck when I was accepted to buy a new baby bulldog. Normally you have to wait for a while as they are quite rare, but when I told the woman my story, she decided to push me forward on the list.

We went to pick up our new baby and when we made the first payment I could not believe the name of the account: Charmaine Robinson. Rebmen's surname was Robinson!

I knew that we may have picked the best dog ever and it was proven on our next visit. When he heard our voices, this tiny puppy ran toward us immediately.

Yes, spirit had come through again. We were not able to pick him up until he was eight weeks old. This would be after our first leg of tours for 2009. One of the interesting things I have found since choosing our dog, is a particular program on television called 'The Dog Whisperer' with a Mexican man, Cesar Milan, as the trainer in the program. This show has helped us understand our dog very well. I have also found he has the same simple message as every spiritual master I have ever come across in my search for answers about being spiritual and creating a balanced life. His message is to watch your dogs and notice how they stay in the moment. He points out frequently that dogs, unlike humans, really do not remember or even care about the past. Dogs feed off the energy in their environment. When fear arises out of a situation triggering a negative memory in us, our dogs being in the moment, will sense it and will immediately take on the same energy.

If we remain calm and assertive in all situations, then whoever is around us will also be more likely to stay calm and assertive, animals and humans alike.

This is the same for very small children. They also have no need for the past or worry about the future. Quite often parents tell me that their two-year-olds are able to give the names and details relating to a deceased family member they have never met or who died before they were born.

Most mothers interpret this as them holding the next and best medium right there in their arms. I hate to disappoint, but your child is simply living in the moment and reacting to the signs, feelings and messages that are constantly coming from spirit. When they start school and are forced to remember the lessons from the previous day, and take on the responsibility of being a good student, the ability to stay in the moment is lost. It may or may not return; only time will tell.

Too many parents however, want me to teach their seven and eight-year-olds how to regain the magic they once possessed. Too many parents want messages from spirits on tap. Unfortunately, this is akin to pushing your child into sports or beauty pageants. The child will eventually either rebel against it or else manipulate the situation for his or her own benefit. My advice is to appreciate it while you can, and try to learn from your children how to stay in the moment. Then you too may receive the very same messages...

In February of 2009, we toured Townsville, Mackay and Rockhampton. It was a tough time in Australia then, floods had just ravished far North Queensland and fires had destroyed some small regional towns in Victoria. We were not sure how we would fare but set out with a newfound determination. I decided to make a donation from the sales of my books and pins to the bushfire fund, and we managed to raise a lot of money. North Queensland turned out in full force for us and I must say that after such a rough ending to the previous year, it felt lovely to have so many people support what I was doing. We went home exhausted but happy and finally claimed our new puppy, Miller. I could feel my injured heart starting to heal the moment he did his first pee on the tiles.

After the first tour, we headed for Western Australia for the very first time. We needed help with the promotion. We had three possible candidates for the position, but when I listened to my heart, I decided to go with Justine, a lovely young woman who was just starting her first business.

Life was good again; there was no doubt about it. I have a great team working with me: Patrick, Justine, Debbie and Trevor. I have been especially lucky in getting Fontaine Press to have faith in my first book 'Spirit Whispers,' republishing it as one of their own. Fontaine have been kind and considerate and their efforts commendable in getting 'Spirit Whispers' on the shelves of bookstores all over Australia. I cannot tell you the amount of emails I have received from people who have found 'Spirit Whispers' in their local bookshop and are now finding something helpful within the pages.

I also have a team on the spirit side, including Crystal, Martin, Dad, Mum and Rebmen, plus countless others. I have been lucky. I have a brand new puppy and I am living in a beautiful house close to my sons. Finally, I have everything I need and everyone I love near me.

My work is fulfilling me in more ways than I can say. I have worked hard, and in such a short amount of time, it seems that I have achieved more than I could have dreamed of. Working in a country as wonderful and spiritually open as Australia is a real blessing. The courage of the producers of 'The One' has paid off and opened the minds of even more people. In the past three years since the completion of my first book, my knowledge of spirit and the healing it provides has multiplied by a thousand.

Chapter 38

With all the work that I've done so far, I've realised that I've been steered towards working with grieving parents. I've found that my own experience of having lost a child has given me a deeper understanding and a unique perspective that many mediums don't share; as well as a very deep realisation that taking the wrong path in the face of such devastating tragedy can almost destroy you.

When I lost Crystal, I turned to alcohol. Far from making the world easier to deal with, it made it an even harder place to be in, creating bigger problems than the already large one I was desperately trying to avoid. Only now, over 20 years later, do I realise that instead of avoiding my grief, I should have tried to learn and grow from it, which I didn't do for many years.

Even after the birth of my first son and the sunshine he brought into my life, I didn't forgive myself for many years for Crystal's death. I kept turning to the bottle when life got a bit rough, as this is how I started dealing with my grief and my problems, even though it had never worked. It took my guides to teach me how to forgive myself, and how to remove myself a little from the situation so I could view it all from a universal, spiritual perspective.

I know now that embracing spirit and accepting the death of a child, no matter how painful or hard, will open up a world of new experiences. No matter how hard things are now, they will always get better.

The passing of my daughter was sudden and tragic, but whatever the circumstances, it is never easy or bearable. I have met far too many parents with vacant eyes and broken hearts to think otherwise. I have done my best to heal their hearts and fill their eyes with hope again. In gratitude, many of them have offered to share their stories hoping that someone will resonate with them. Their story of grief and tragedy may propel someone like you forward in search of your own spirit children. It may make your own tragic loss seem a little more rational, and they realise that sharing their story with the intention of love and healing will also help them on their own journey. I know it has been a healing process for my bereaved parents. It has taken many hours of talking and sharing to bring their tales to life and allow you to receive the full picture. It has been healing for us all and has humbled me to be in the presence of such strength and courage. I am grateful for the input of these parents and I know that many of you are in awe of their strength. I know the parents depicted in this book are at a place of acceptance, or else their stories would not be here. They realise that life goes on and so must they.

No matter how many times you say 'what if this' and 'if only that', the death you are grieving is a reality and nothing is going to change that. No matter how many times you tell yourself they were too young, that they had their whole life ahead of them, nothing can change the cruel reality many of you are facing. The one you love has finished their physical life and is now residing in spirit. No matter what, the time they died was always going to be the time they died. It was not too soon nor was it too late; it was their time.

With death comes change, whether we like it or not. The deaths of all the people I love have catapulted me onto a path of spirituality and love I may not have found otherwise. Now you find yourself walking beside me in hope you may learn something to make sense of the losses you have faced. My message is of hope for the living. It comes from the spirit world with love.

The spirit children are watching. Remember that. They are there waiting for you when it is your time to meet them again. They wait with the whole spiritual universe, patiently, while you finish your life contract. They send you messages and love all the time, and the sooner you can raise your vibrations to meet theirs, the sooner you will heal. The sooner you can learn to stay in the present moment and observe the messages coming from nature, music, dreams, numbers, and feelings, the more awake you will become and the more aware of their presence you will be.

I hope this book helps you on your path, and that it is received with the love with which it was intended. I hope you find a story or even a line that gives you the 'light bulb' moment necessary to move through your grief a little easier. Whether you miss a child, a friend or a family member, the message in this book is for everyone who has loved and lost someone to the realm of spirit. Life goes on for eternity, and this life you are living is only a small part of a much bigger picture.

I am a living proof that life goes on. We should strive to live our life with courage, laugh away our tears, and love always, because love will always prevail no matter how far away it seems.

Keep in touch with Charmaine by requesting
her as a friend on Facebook, and visiting her
website: www.charmainewilson.com.au

Sign-up to the Fontaine Press e-newsletter
and be the first to be notified of Charmaine's
next offering (an exciting first for Australia):
www.fontainepress.com/news

FONTAINE
——PRESS——